HF5718

COMMUNICATIONS TOOLKIT

A guide to navigating communications for the nonprofit world

written, designed & published by **cause communications, santa monica**

R. Christine Hershey, Author
Susan L. Wampler, Project Writer/Researcher
Andrew J. Posey, Editor
Joanna Lee, Design Director
Kristin Allen, Designer
Anne M. Perry, Copy Editor
Preeti Narang, Research Assistant

R. Christine Hershey

As president and founder of Hershey Associates and Cause Communications, based in Santa Monica, California, Chris consults with CEOs and senior executives throughout the country, advising on questions of positioning, market strategy and brand identity. Over the past 25 years, Chris has grown Hershey Associates into a nationally recognized design and marketing communications company. Her work in the corporate sector, and her commitment to helping nonprofits succeed, were the catalysts for the creation of Cause Communications, Hershey Associate's 501(c)(3).

Cause Communications

Cause Communications is a nonprofit communications firm that advances the work of foundations and nonprofits through communications that reach, inspire and motivate. Cause Communications applies many of the same communications strategies Fortune 500 companies use to succeed. Our knowledge comes from the expertise gained from Cause Communications' sister company, Hershey Associates, whose clients include AT&T, the Walt Disney Co. and Wells Fargo. For more information, visit www.causecommunications.org.

This guide was developed by nonprofits for nonprofits, for educational purposes only. We are grateful to all our contributors. No part of this book may be reproduced in any form without written permission from the publisher.

Copyright ©2005 Cause Communications. All rights reserved.
ISBN 0-9763027-1-3
Library of Congress Control Number: 2004116709

This book was made possible through the support of:
The Annenberg Foundation
The California Endowment
The James Irvine Foundation
Marguerite Casey Foundation

Printed in Hong Kong

www.causecommunications.org • Santa Monica • 310.458.2823

table of contents

Acknowledgments

INTRODUCTION
- Why communications and why now?
- Defining communications
- Lessons from the corporate world
- The research that informed this book
- How to use this book

CHAPTER ONE – WHERE ARE YOU NOW?........1
Research Basics 2
- Qualitative vs. quantitative research
- Primary research on a shoestring
- Free research
- Four steps in the survey process

Research Tools 4
- Focus groups – the basics
- Communications audits
- Sample audit questions
- Even the scales

Competitive Analysis 6
- Sources and trends
- Competitive analysis, the Tom Peters method
- What you need to know about your peers

CHAPTER TWO – WHERE DO YOU WANT TO GO?........9
Communications Plan 10
- Crisis communications
- Tying your communications plan to your mission
- Targeting your audience
- Elements of a communications plan

Branding 12
- Brand essentials
- The difference between a brand and a logo
- Determining a nonprofit's brand value

Identity 14
- Great logos
- Logo test questions
- Do-it-yourself guide to re-evaluating your identity
- Creating a style guide

Message Development 16
- Great slogans
- Six-point checklist for evaluating your slogan
- Storytelling
- Seven questions to sharpen your stories
- Messages that stick
- Eliminating jargon

i

table of contents

CHAPTER THREE – HOW DO WE GET THERE? 19

Creating a Budget 20
- Stretching limited dollars
- Budget checklist

Finding Funds 22
- Lessons from the corporate sector
- Add communications to all grant requests
- Find corporate partners
- Identify "friends"

Selling It 24
- Watch your language

Hiring Help: Staff or Consultant? 26
- Hiring help
- Six good reasons to hire a consultant
- Tips for working with consultants
- No one can do it all

Collaborating 28
- Evaluating potential partners
- Cause-related marketing
- Media sponsorships

CHAPTER FOUR – WHAT TO TAKE 31

Advertising 32
- Seven print-ad principles
- Public service announcements
- Paying to be heard
- Online advertising

Advocacy 34
- Shaping policy: what you may and may not do
- Calling legislators
- Writing letters
- Five essential steps in an advocacy campaign

Capital Campaigns 36
- Ask your donors
- Producing an effective case statement
- Feasibility study topics
- Key campaign communications vehicles

Direct Mail 38
- Direct mail do's and don'ts
- Attracting planned gifts
- Maintaining an accurate database
- Timing your solicitation

Donor Cultivation and Grant Writing 40
- The three "C's" of prospect research
- Stewardship strategies
- Producing effective proposals
- Seven thank yous

Electronic Media 42
- Viral marketing do's
- Getting your message through

table of contents

Events 44
- Leverage the impact of your events
- Star-struck or star-stuck?
- Top speechwriting tips

Guerilla Marketing 46
- Some guerilla tactics

Marketing Materials 48
- Getting the most from your publications
- Low-budget, high-impact ideas
- Push vs. pull
- Print and Web publishing pluses and minuses

Media Relations 50
- Working with the media
- Ethnic and gay/lesbian media
- Components of a media relations plan
- Tracking your coverage
- Who do you call?

Media: Pitching Your Story 52
- Who to pitch?
- When to pitch?
- E-mail, fax or snail mail?
- Building a media list
- Media alerts

Web Sites: Creating and Maintaining 54
- Web sites – seven common mistakes
- Testing your site
- To blog or not to blog
- Great Web sites

Web Sites: Optimization 56
- Seven key factors in search-engine optimization
- Using listservs
- Online giving

CHAPTER FIVE – ARE WE THERE YET? 59

Measurement 60
- Tools for measuring results

Refining/Adjusting 62
- Keys to effective evaluation
- The power of communications

Looking Ahead 65

Index 66

Pocket Inserts/Templates
- Cost-and-benefit chart of select media
- Creative brief
- Event-planning checklist
- News release guidelines
- Photo/video release form
- Sample campaign style guide
- Sample communications survey
- Sample identity guidelines
- SWOT analysis form

Introduction

We believe in the power of nonprofits to transform our society. And we believe in the power of well-crafted communications to transform nonprofits. Effective communications can target the right messages to the right audiences at the right times. And an investment in appropriate, well-planned communications can increase rather than detract from the bottom line when resources and staffing are tight.

In our consulting practice, we routinely field calls from nonprofits on questions about communications that are as varied as the organizations themselves. What they have in common, though, is the need to find the most effective ways of raising awareness and raising funds.

We found many books, workshops and tapes available on individual aspects of nonprofit communications, but no single source that covered a broad spectrum of nonprofit communications needs. We also found no current research that speaks to what tools nonprofit communicators need or want.

> National qualitative and quantitative research ensured the content of this toolkit was **DIRECTED** by the people it was intended to serve.

To determine the tools you use and what you want to learn more about, we conducted national qualitative and quantitative surveys with small, medium and large nonprofits. The result is a book whose content was directed by the people it was intended to serve.

This book is intended as a guide to help you find the best approaches, messages and vehicles for reaching all of your key audiences. It is not meant to be a textbook or definitive source on any one topic, but rather an overview of what you, as a nonprofit leader, need to know to navigate your way through myriad communications efforts — from branding your organization and developing your communications plan to choosing the right approaches and measuring your results.

We've borrowed ideas from the corporate world, including our own corporate consulting practice. We know from experience that by using the same techniques *Fortune 500* companies employ, we can help nonprofits achieve even greater results.

We also received invaluable assistance from the philanthropic community. Throughout the entire process, we have found them to be supportive, receptive and anxious to bring this type of resource to you. Specifically, we would like to thank The Annenberg Foundation, The California Endowment, The James Irvine Foundation and Marguerite Casey Foundation for their support, wise counsel and encouragement.

WHY COMMUNICATIONS AND WHY NOW?

Nonprofits typically have two main goals for their communications programs – raising awareness and raising funds. Yet getting your messages heard and moving people to act have never been more challenging, or more important.

Each day, consumers are bombarded with some 3,000 advertising messages, according to *The Economist* (June 2004). With all that information clutter, how do you make your organization stand out?

In the corporate world, not being visible eventually means going out of business. And more nonprofits are coming to understand that the same is true in the nonprofit sector. If those you are trying to serve don't know you exist, or if donors don't understand that you need their support, your organization's survival can be at risk.

"In a crowded marketplace…not standing out is the same as being invisible," says marketing guru Seth Godin in his book *Purple Cow: Transform Your Business by Being Remarkable*.

Today, nonprofits face increased scrutiny from government agencies and the public regarding their governance and financial standards.

> ### defining communications
>
> If you search Google for "communications," you get everything from telecommunications to couples counseling. If you look in the dictionary, you'll find several definitions, including "the art and technique of using words effectively to impart information or ideas" (*American Heritage Dictionary of the English Language: Fourth Edition*, 2000). That's close. But the truth is that everything you do – or don't do – communicates a message to your audience, whether it's those you serve, your volunteers, donors, staff, the media or the government.

Proactive communications strategies can stave off potential crises while positioning a nonprofit as a worthy recipient of support and of the public trust.

To get your messages heard, understood and remembered, you need to use some of the same channels and strategies that for-profits use.

LESSONS FROM THE CORPORATE WORLD

Corporate America spends some $263 billion each year to convince consumers to buy their products and services. They make the investment because communications, in the form of advertising, public relations, direct mail and the like, motivate people to act. If they didn't work and if bigger sales and bigger profits weren't the result, corporations wouldn't budget for these communications efforts.

While it's not realistic, or even desirable, for the nonprofit sector to match corporate spending dollar for dollar, nonprofits can learn countless lessons from the corporate world about how to get the biggest return possible on their investment in communications.

For instance, nonprofits often consider market research a luxury they cannot afford. But to effectively reach the right audience with the right message, you not only need research, but you also need to target your audiences precisely. Corporations like Procter & Gamble or General Electric don't market to "women." They market to "second-generation Latinas living in Atlanta, who are married, between the ages of 35 and 40, have three children, care for their monolingual parents and have a dual income of $75,000."

Research doesn't have to be expensive, though. We've devoted Chapter One of this book to the subject and have included numerous tips for conducting relevant and useful research on a shoestring budget.

Similarly, many nonprofits believe that developing a strong, well-defined brand and organizational identity is only for the Coca-Colas, General Motors and Microsofts of the world, and not relevant to nonprofits. But building a recognizable, trustworthy brand is crucial to attracting and retaining a base of donors who will support your cause year in and year out. Chapter Two delves into these issues, as well as the importance of communications planning and messaging.

Chapter Three covers budgeting, collaborating with external partners and getting your board to support an investment in your communications efforts. Here, the lessons from the corporate world are even more dramatic. Pharmaceutical companies frequently spend up to twice as much on overhead, marketing, promotion and advertising as they spend on research and development of new drugs, according to the *Los Angeles Times*. In the entertainment industry, the average cost of producing a film in 2003 was $63.8 million, while the cost of marketing was $39 million – an increase of 28 percent from the prior year. These industries, and others throughout the corporate sphere, devote serious budget dollars to communications because of the powerful impact marketing has on the bottom line.

Nonprofits increasingly are using traditionally corporate strategies to generate increased revenues. For example, Goodwill Industries attributes double-digit sales increases to a national advertising campaign it launched early in 2004, and *The New York Times* recently reported that nonprofit advertising budgets increased by 15.8 percent between 2002 and 2003. Chapter Four not only discusses this and other trends, but also focuses on the spectrum of communications tools available to nonprofits and how and when to best use them.

Chapter Five addresses measuring your communications efforts to ensure maximum return on investment. Here, too, the corporate world provides a useful model. Successful

| Nike corporate slogan | Nike slogan, if written by a nonprofit executive |

JUST DO IT!

"While an occasional disinclination to exercise is exhibited by all age cohorts, the likelihood of positive health outcomes makes even mildly strenuous physical activity all the more imperative."

Source: Andy Goodman, free-range thinking, November 2003

corporations systematically track audience perceptions before *and* after implementing a communications effort – an approach that would both help nonprofit communicators better quantify the results of their hard work and help educate their boards that communications has a definite return on investment.

THE RESEARCH THAT INFORMED THIS BOOK

In developing this book, we followed our own advice, to first research the audiences we sought to assist – nonprofits across the country with communications budgets ranging from miniscule to seven figures – and find out what was important to them.

First, we conducted a qualitative audit – lasting from 30 minutes to an hour per person – with 150 nonprofit executive directors and senior communications staff nationwide. Our questions were open-ended to allow people to talk freely about the communications vehicles they're using now and the types of tools they'd like to know more about.

While the qualitative audit gave us specific directives and excellent anecdotal information, we also tested our initial findings with a quantitative audit. We constructed a national quantitative audit and sent it to 3,000 individuals in nonprofits of various sizes. We received more than 300 responses, giving us a ± 4.9 percent sampling error with a 95 percent confidence level. This offered us the statistical accuracy needed to confirm findings and direct the content and structure of this book. Not only does this make the book unique, but we also hope it becomes a resource that you and your staff will enjoy using.

HOW TO USE THIS BOOK

This book covers a diverse range of communications vehicles for nonprofits. Most nonprofits will use some, but not all, of the tools described in these pages. For some organizations, funding communications is a low priority, not by choice, but by necessity. We've therefore included tips for organizations on a shoestring budget.

As we've said, this book does not pretend to be all you need to know on any one subject, but rather, an overview of tips, tools and resources.

Throughout the book, you will find:
- "Survey Says" blocks indicating what we have heard through our research. We use percentages when referring to the quantitative results and terms like "majority" and "few" when referring to the qualitative findings.
- "Roadside Assistance" blocks listing additional resources so you can find more material on the section you're reading.
- Colorful half-page inserts highlighting "do's and don'ts" and "best of" tips.

And in the back pocket you will find actual samples, templates and forms you are free to use.

It is our hope that this toolkit will serve as a helpful resource, one that you will refer to often.

And please let us know your thoughts. We plan to update the content regularly, so your feedback will help us ensure that future editions continue to reflect the most current communications needs of the nonprofit sector. Please forward your comments to toolkit@causecommunications.org.

chapter one
where are you now?

In order to know where your organization should go, you need to know where you are right now. Research takes the guesswork out of your communications program. It gives you concrete evidence of how your organization is perceived, including whether the perceptions of those inside your organization match those of your key audiences.

Are your publications highly valued and read? Is your Web site easy to navigate? Do your direct-mail appeals include an effective call to action? Research will help you answer these questions and will give you the evidence you need to allocate your limited communications budgets wisely.

In this chapter, we'll cover a variety of research strategies and tools and how to use them effectively in planning and evaluating your communications efforts.

research basics: start at the beginning

survey says: 90% OF YOU DO NOT CONDUCT RESEARCH.

RESEARCH is one of the most important and valuable steps in the development of any communications initiative. Nonprofits often shy away from conducting such research out of concern that it will be too costly and/or too complicated, but it doesn't have to be.

Research is crucial in establishing a baseline for measuring the success of your efforts and in reducing the risk of lost time and money that often comes with even the most educated assumptions. And it often yields unexpected results, even happy surprises, such as learning that your donors would prefer to receive an electronic version of your expensive printed annual report.

> Research often establishes a baseline for measuring the success of your efforts.

There are two basic kinds of research: primary and secondary. Primary research is information you gather yourself or commission to have done.

Primary research can be as simple as asking, via phone, e-mail, direct mail or in person, and then listening to the feedback (see the sidebar "Primary research on a shoestring" for a few cost-saving strategies).

Secondary research uses existing information already published in print, on the Internet or through external sources such as the media, libraries, universities, trade associations and government agencies.

Primary research is invaluable for testing materials and messages. Surveying your audience, or conducting focus groups, can help you make any necessary modifications before you invest significant funds in printing an expensive direct-mail solicitation or launch a new Web site.

Pros of secondary research are that it's free and available everywhere. Cons are that it may not be exactly what you're looking for and can be time-intensive to find. ■

qualitative vs. quantitative research

Qualitative research allows people to share emotions, explain their thoughts, confirm areas of concern and uncover topics the organization may not know are hot-button issues. Qualitative techniques include focus groups (both live and online), one-on-one meetings and phone calls.

By their nature, qualitative interviews are information-rich and time-intensive. However, as all responses vary, and sample size is not always large enough to give you the statistical accuracy needed, you may need to tabulate your results with terms like "most," "the majority" or "average."

Quantitative research generally is used for larger groups and it measures, in numeric terms, what people think. Quantitative interviews have uniform questions, with uniform responses, that enable a researcher to easily capture and tabulate results. However, this format does tend to limit the amount of open-ended information you can collect.

Typical quantitative research techniques include surveys using the telephone, the Internet or the mail. Depending on the number of people you survey, quantitative surveys provide a specific level of statistical accuracy. This type of research can confirm or refute findings uncovered through qualitative research.

primary research on a shoestring

Here are a few low-cost ideas for conducting your own primary research:

- For less than $50 in stamps and stationery, you can send a survey to 100 people asking for their feedback on a particular publication, direct-mail piece or other communications vehicle.
- Gather a dozen of your most important constituents for an informal focus group (providing simple refreshments such as coffee, juice and cookies) for input on your organization's new logo.
- Invest a few hours of staff time to call a targeted group of audience members to answer a phone survey about your organization and your communications efforts.
- A number of companies offer e-mail and Web survey templates and services, which can be quick and cost-effective. Some, such as www.zoomerang.com, offer discounts to nonprofits.
- Another audience research technique is to create a chat room on your Web site where constituents can share and exchange feedback about your organization. It's an inexpensive and effective way to obtain research on what your audiences think about you.
- Convince a donor to underwrite a major quantitative research survey.

see sample communications survey in the back pocket

free research

One of the best places to look for free information is, of course, the Internet. Following are a few sources of readily available research:

- www.fedstats.gov – portal for locating government statistics
- www.census.gov/sdc/www – State Data Centers, where you can find median age and household income by zip code
- www.profusion.com – search multiple sources simultaneously
- www.marketresearch.com – a comprehensive collection of published market research
- Google and other search engines
- University libraries and research centers – an often overlooked but invaluable source of free research

four steps in the survey process

- Identify your target audience.
- Develop the questionnaire.
- Conduct the survey.
- Analyze the information.

roadside assistance

Research Design: Qualitative, Quantitative and Mixed Methods Approaches
by John W. Creswell (2002)

An Introduction to Statistical Methods and Data Analysis
by R. Lyman Ott (2001)

The Market Research Toolbox
by Edward F. McQuarrie (1996)

Transforming Qualitative Data: Description, Analysis and Interpretation
by Harry F. Wolcott (1994)

research tools

survey says: MORE THAN HALF OF YOU DON'T CONSIDER AUDITS RELEVANT TO YOUR WORK.

SURVEYS and focus groups are the key primary research implements in your toolkit. You may want to conduct surveys for a wide variety of purposes, from the comprehensive communications audit, which provides feedback on the effectiveness of your entire communications program, to questionnaires about specific communications vehicles or issues.

Marketing expert Harry Beckwith says that phone surveys often provide better results than mail or in-person surveys. "Time after time, oral surveys work better," he says. "It's physically easier to talk than to write. So people say more in oral surveys than they write on written ones. Phone surveys usually produce more revealing results than in-person surveys. On the phone, people will open up and reveal the information you need." And, according to Entrepreneur.com, phone surveys cost about one-third the price of in-person interviews. They also tend to be less expensive than mail surveys, except for particularly large survey audiences.

> Your audience gives you everything you **NEED.** They tell you. There is no director who can direct you like an audience.
> comedian fanny brice

You can increase the effectiveness of your mail surveys by notifying the audience in advance, by phone or by postcard, that the survey is coming. If you are conducting a survey about an existing publication, it is often a good idea to send a copy of the publication along with the survey to refresh readers' memories (unless you are seeking feedback on their unaided recollection of your publication's contents). A much-less-expensive way of reminding readers is to include a thumbnail photo of the cover of your publication on the questionnaire.

No matter what tool you use, you need to spend a considerable amount of time and thought on developing your questionnaire. The quality of the questionnaire is key to the success of your effort, whether it's a comprehensive communications audit, a questionnaire about your newsletter or a focus group review of your new graphic identity program (i.e., a new organizational logo, colors, letterhead system, etc.). Consider testing the questions on a small group to surface potential problems with your questionnaire before you poll your full audience. ■

communications audits

Communications audits provide a thorough analysis of your nonprofit's internal and external communications and also let you know where you stand in relation to your peer organizations. An audit can help you learn if your messages are getting through to, and resonating with, your key audiences, and it can also help you identify the most effective communications vehicle to address any gaps. Ask the right questions of the right audiences and use the information you glean to inform your communications plan.

Audits generally are more effective if conducted by an outsider. Consultants can be more objective than longtime staff, and participants often are more comfortable speaking freely with someone not employed by the organization. Audits should be conducted whenever there is a major change in your organization, such as a new CEO, major affiliation or crisis.

sample audit questions

Audit questions should be tailored for each audience you are surveying. Following are some ideas to get you started:

1. What do you think is most unique about ABC nonprofit organization?
2. Where do you usually first hear or see news/changes at ABC nonprofit?
3. Are you happy with how news/changes are communicated to you from ABC nonprofit?
4. What is your attitude toward ABC nonprofit?
5. What sense do you have of ABC nonprofit's reputation in the community?
6. What is ABC nonprofit best known for?
7. For you, what is the most compelling reason to support ABC nonprofit?
8. Do you have any reasons for not wanting to support ABC nonprofit?
9. Do ABC nonprofit's advertising and communications stand out from the competition?
10. Are ABC nonprofit's products and services clearly identifiable?
11. Are you familiar with ABC nonprofit's current marketing campaign? What do you think about it?
12. Are there other issues regarding ABC nonprofit and its plans that you would like to raise?

even the scales

When you ask an audience to rate a project or program, use a scale with an even number of choices. For instance, if you use a scale of 1-5, you will tend to get an abundance of "3"s. But if ask people to rate on a scale of 1-4, you'll get a better idea of their real opinions, since no "neutral" choice is available.

roadside assistance

Listening to Your Donors: The Nonprofit's Practical Guide to Designing and Conducting Surveys
by Bruce Campbell (2000)

Focus Groups: A Practical Guide for Applied Research
by Richard Krueger and Mary Anne Casey (2000)

Selling the Invisible: A Field Guide to Modern Marketing
by Harry Beckwith (1997)

Conducting Successful Focus Groups
by Judith Sharken Simon (1999)
(available through www.wilder.org)

competitive analysis

survey says: ONLY 20% OF YOU KNOW WHAT YOUR PEERS OR DONOR COMPETITORS ARE DOING IN THE AREA OF COMMUNICATIONS.

ONCE you have a clear understanding of the perception your constituents have of your organization, you also need to know where you stand in relation to other organizations with whom you vie for media attention and donor support. This critical phase of your research is called competitive analysis, and it helps determine who your peer institutions are, how they are perceived, where they are heading, what audiences they serve and, most importantly, what distinguishes your organization from theirs.

Your approach can be formal, with a team of consultants conducting extensive quantitative research and building a "war room" of samples from your peer institutions that you can compare side by side. Or you can take the informal, bare-bones route by gathering all the materials you can get your hands on and making a few phone calls to conduct a quick survey. Either way, competitive analysis is crucial to building a strong identity for your organization.

> Success means never letting the competition define you. Instead, you have to **DEFINE** yourself based on a point of view you care deeply about.
> tom chappell, tom's of maine

Management guru Tom Peters boils it down to two simple questions: Who are you and why are you here? A big part of the "who are you" question is determining what makes you unique. What do you do that no one else can do? And one of the best ways to answer that crucial question is to look at how you compare with institutions that serve the same core constituency. The "why are you here" question is about having a clear, focused mission that resonates with your constituents. ■

sources and trends

Check out trends in the nonprofit sector, learn what your peers are doing and gain access to valuable employment, technology, communications and other valuable resources by bookmarking these sites:

- www.foundationcenter.org – The Foundation Center offers information (some free, some fee-based) about the nation's philanthropic foundations.
- www.guidestar.org – GuideStar provides financial information (including IRS Form 990) on some 800,000 nonprofits. Much of the information is free, but the site also offers fee-based information, including "Salary Search," a resource for nonprofit salaries.
- www.philanthropy.com – *The Chronicle of Philanthropy* covers trends and news in the nonprofit world and publishes job listings, grant opportunities and more. Subscribers to the weekly paper get even more from the Web site, including access to the paper's archives and "The Nonprofit Handbook."
- www.idealist.org – Idealist posts nonprofit job openings, volunteer opportunities and internships, as well as consultants.
- www.techsoup.org – Techsoup contains a wealth of technology information and case studies aimed at nonprofits. It also connects nonprofits with donated and discounted technology products from providers including Cisco and Microsoft.
- www.comnetwork.org – The Communications Network is dedicated to strengthening the voice of philanthropy; its site contains a variety of communications tools.
- www.charitynavigator.org – Charity Navigator is America's largest independent evaluator of charities. It offers a variety of top-10 lists and facts about the nonprofit sector.
- www.networkforgood.org – Network for Good is a nonprofit collaboration to help organizations increase capacity, reach new audiences and build Internet strategies.
- www.ephilanthropy.org – ePhilanthropyFoundation.org fosters secure, private and ethical online philanthropy.
- www.firstgov.gov – FirstGov for Nonprofits is a federal government portal to information for nonprofits.
- www.irs.gov/charities – This Internal Revenue Service site contains tax information for charities and other nonprofits.
- www.inkindex.com – Inkindex is an online resource that facilitates the donation of excess corporate inventory to nonprofit organizations.
- www.boardsource.org – Board Source is dedicated to increasing the effectiveness of nonprofit organizations by strengthening boards of directors.
- www.whatworks.org – The Center for What Works aims to improve performance in the nonprofit sector and focuses on benchmarking.

what you need to know about your peers

1. What are their goals?
2. Who are their constituents?
3. What are their key messages?
4. How are they perceived?
5. What works for them and what doesn't?

see SWOT analysis form in the back pocket

competitive analysis, the Tom Peters method

Try this exercise to determine how you differ from your peers:

- Who are we? (one page, then 25 words)
- List three ways in which we are unique to our [constituents].
- Who are they [peer institutions]? (identify in 25 words)
- List three distinct "us"/"them" differences.
- Try results on your teammates.
- Try them on a friend.
- Try them on a skeptic.

Source: Tom Peters, www.tompeters.com

Tom Peters is the co-author of the groundbreaking *In Search of Excellence* and many subsequent business books.

roadside assistance

Purple Cow: Transform Your Business by Being Remarkable
by Seth Godin (2003)

Differentiate or Die: Survival in Our Era of Killer Competition
by Jack Trout and Steve Rivkin (2000)

The Circle of Innovation
by Tom Peters (1999)

Built to Last: Successful Habits of Visionary Companies
by James C. Collins and Jerry I. Porras (1997)

Competitive Strategy
by Michael E. Porter (1998)

TOP TIPS

- Know your audiences and continuously seek their feedback.

- Conduct communications audits of your internal and external communications periodically.

- Test your materials and messages before you unveil them publicly.

- Know your peer institutions as well as you know your own organization.

chapter two
where do you want to go?

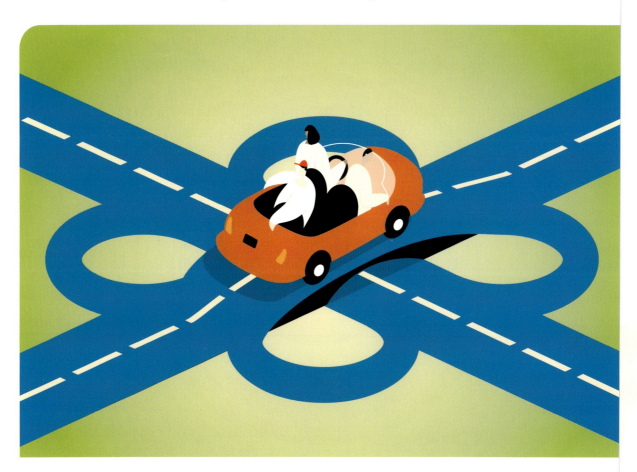

If you know where you are going and what you hope to accomplish for your organization through your communications efforts, it becomes much easier to plan the most efficient and appropriate route. So your starting point is really your destination. Consider what success would physically look like and then work backward to develop a plan of action to get you there.

How do you want your target audience to perceive your organization? What actions do you want them to take?

In this chapter, we'll show you how to develop a communications plan, what to do in an emergency, how to create a strong brand and visual identity for your institution, and how to develop and frame key messages to drive it all home.

communications plan: a roadmap

survey says: 57% OF YOU RATE KNOWLEDGE OF CRISIS COMMUNICATIONS AS VITAL OR VERY USEFUL YET MOST DON'T HAVE AN ORGANIZED, TESTED PLAN.

YOUR ORGANIZATION'S mission and the research you've conducted are the starting points for developing your strategic communications plan. Ideally, your plan should be linked to your organization's overall strategic direction. At the least, it must define your unique position in the market and frame your organization and its key issues in a way that resonates with your audiences.

> The indispensable first step to getting the things you want out of life is this: **DECIDE** what you want.
> author and comedian ben stein

In writing your communications plan, avoid generic goals such as "raise awareness" or "increase media coverage." Be specific. Which audience do you want to make aware of your organization – community leaders, those you want to serve, prospective donors? Even if it's all of the above, you need to segment those audiences and develop strategies to effectively reach each target group. What actions do you want your audiences to take?

Your goals must be measurable. If you run a theater company and your goal is to boost attendance, state how many people you want to attract. If you want more media coverage, identify the number and quality of placements (e.g., one placement each month in major national media).

Now it's time for a reality check. Do your goals match your available resources? Are you being realistic about what you can achieve and how much it will cost? Do you have the wherewithal to support the increased volume if your communications efforts are wildly successful?

Be prepared for success. Many campaigns fail because of implementation issues; an overwhelmed call center, faulty business-reply cards, ineffective donor tracking. Be ready. Think through all of the steps, from developing your concept to reaching your intended audience. For instance, don't forget to include a distribution plan for your print materials. If you've gone to the trouble and expense of creating an annual report or a newsletter, make sure the publication gets into people's hands and doesn't just sit in boxes.

Don't forget to include your Web site and electronic communications in your communications planning. An October 2004 report by *The NonProfit Times* revealed that 92 percent of nonprofits polled in its survey had a Web site, but only 24 percent had a written online strategy. ■

tying your communications plan to your mission

Since your ultimate goal is fulfilling your organization's philanthropic mission, your communications plan must be inextricably linked to your mission to keep you on course. Try the following exercise to help keep your communications plan mission-focused:

Ask yourself what the successful fulfillment of your mission would look like. Then ask what communications tools you will need at the macro level to make that possible. For instance, if your organization's mission is to cure heart disease, your macro communications efforts would probably focus on educating those at risk and raising money for research. To educate those at risk, you might launch a national awareness campaign, produce a newsletter and/or host a health fair. To develop those programs, you would need to allocate financial and human resources, develop a timetable, and so on. Keep delving until you have a comprehensive implementation plan that is driven by your mission.

targeting your audience

In the 2004 presidential election campaign, George W. Bush and John Kerry both relied heavily on television advertising but targeted vastly different shows for their messages. President Bush relied on shows such as *Cops, Law and Order* and *JAG,* while Senator Kerry turned to programming such as *Late Show with David Letterman, The Ellen DeGeneres Show* and *Judge Judy*.

"Those choices do not reflect either man's taste in television, but critical differences in the advertising strategies of their campaigns, which [spent] more money for commercials than any other campaigns in presidential history," wrote Jim Rutenberg in a July 2004 article in *The New York Times*.

Crime shows attracted the Republican men Bush wanted to reach, while the Kerry ad campaign focused on single women, according to an extensive study produced by the Wisconsin Advertising Project and Nielsen Monitor-Plus, the first time the Nielsen television-rating organization has tracked presidential advertising in all 210 TV markets it measures.

see cost-and-benefit chart of select media in the back pocket

elements of a communications plan

- Summary/overview of plan
- Goals (general)/objectives (specific)
- Target audiences
- Key messages
- Strategies (approaches)/ tactics (tools)
- Budget
- Implementation plan with accountabilities, priorities and timetable
- Evaluation (what success would look like)

> I don't know the key to success, but the **KEY** to failure is trying to please everybody.
> comedian bill cosby

Be sure you have:
- A clear tie to your organization's strategic goals
- Specificity about target audience and desired response
- Flexibility to respond to market changes

roadside assistance

Harvard Business Review: Crisis Management (2000)

Crisis Management, Planning for the Inevitable by Steven Fink (2000)

Ongoing Crisis Communication: Planning, Managing, & Responding by W. Timothy Coombs (1999)

The PR Crisis Bible: Take Charge of the Media When All Hell Breaks Loose by Robin Cohn (2000)

branding

survey says: 84% OF YOU RATE BRANDING ACTIVITIES AS VITAL OR VERY USEFUL.

WHETHER you know it or not, your organization already has a brand identity. It's everything the world sees and hears about you – how your phones are answered, how staff presents itself, how your materials look, how your Web site works. And, more importantly, it's how your audiences perceive your organization based on all those factors and then some.

"Anyone who wants to build a great brand first has to understand who they are," says Scott Bedbury, who ran the brand-building campaigns for Nike and Starbucks and co-authored *A New Brand World*. "The real starting point is to go out to consumers and find out what they like or dislike about the brand and what they associate as the very core of the brand concept."

Branding is not just for big corporations. It's a necessity for nonprofits as well. At its essence, branding is about establishing meaningful relationships with your audience and building trust in your organization.

> A brand is a living **ENTITY**, and it is enriched or undermined cumulatively over time, the product of a thousand small gestures.
> michael eisner, disney ceo

Your brand is your organization's DNA. It's what makes you tick, what makes your organization unique, what makes you worthy of support. Think of your brand as your promise to your stakeholders both internal and external.

Your brand is your most powerful tool for strengthening your organization from the inside out. When you clarify and communicate what you stand for inside your nonprofit, you instill not only a sense of pride but also a motivational tool for your staff and volunteers to live the promise in their day-to-day tasks. And when all levels of your staff are dedicated to fulfilling the brand promise, your key audiences can't help but notice.

Remember, you already have a brand. Proactively managing it helps distinguish you from other institutions, brings consistency and focus to all your communications and services, and builds trust and support among your stakeholders. ■

brand essentials

The following are essential components of a strong brand identity:

- Agreement among your board and senior leadership about the importance of developing and maintaining a consistent brand.
- Sufficient allocation of resources – time, talent and money – toward building your organization's brand.
- Relevance of your brand to the audiences you want to reach.
- Consistency in your messages.
- Consistency in your materials.
- Consistency in how employees and volunteers at all levels portray your organization.
- Consistent follow-through on your organization's promises, direct and implied, to all of your key audiences.
- Ongoing measurement of whether you are increasing the value of your brand in the eyes of your constituents.

the difference between a brand and a logo

Your graphic identity system – your logo and other visuals – reinforces your brand. It is not the brand. The brand is much larger than that. It is the essence of your organization, the promises you make to your most important audiences and the relationships you build with your constituents. For more on identity programs, turn the page.

determining a nonprofit's brand value

Corporate, or for-profit, brand valuation identifies the profits generated by a brand. This figure can then be used to achieve a wide range of business goals. [Nonprofit] brands, on the other hand, do not have an identifiable profit stream, although they do generate money for their cause. Therefore, a more relevant methodology would be in establishing the value that the brand creates for the cause it supports.

Why would a nonprofit go through the trouble of valuing its brand? Establishing the value of a nonprofit brand can open the door to co-branding, licensing and partnering opportunities. Additionally, it allows one to determine reasonable spending on marketing and offers a point from which to explain the power of the brand.

Brand valuation for nonprofits considers factors such as the public's level of trust that the donation will be used effectively, the public's perception of the organization's financial stability, the public's personal experience with the cause, the organization's level of contact with the donor and the ease of transaction for the donor.

The idea of valuing a nonprofit brand is still quite new to the charitable community. However, some organizations have started to establish a monetary figure for their brand with a view of helping them grow the value further. As an example, Habitat for Humanity International's brand placed at nearly $2 billion in 2001.

Dennis Bender, senior vice president of communications at Habitat for Humanity International, says that his strategy for determining the brand value was to "establish the brand in the context of corporate America and consumer products companies and then to show both leadership and membership what is at stake."

Source: "Do Nonprofits Have Value?" by Robin Rusch, www.brandchannel.com, July 2002

roadside assistance

Bang! Getting Your Message Heard in a Noisy World
by Linda Kaplan Thaler and Robin Koval (2005)

The 22 Immutable Laws of Branding
by Al Ries and Laura Ries (2002)

Brand Leadership
by David A. Aaker and Erich Joachimsthaler (2000)

The Brand Gap
by Marty Neumeier (2003)

Brand Aid
by Brad Van Auken (2003)

www.brandchannel.com

www.allaboutbranding.com

see sample campaign style guide in the back pocket

identity

survey says: 95% OF YOU STRIVE FOR A CONSISTENT LOOK AND FEEL IN YOUR COMMUNICATIONS, YET ONLY 20% USE A STYLE GUIDE OR EMPLOYEE TRAINING TO ENSURE CONSISTENCY.

ONE OF the most important ways in which you differentiate yourself from other institutions is through your organizational identity. It should be distinctive, appropriate, memorable and used consistently.

Your identity is a key component of your brand. It's the images and words that identify you as you. It's the Nike swoosh, the plop-plop fizz-fizz of Alka Seltzer and the bright red of Coke.

Your identity starts with the name of your organization. If possible, your name should reflect your mission. Good examples are Bread for the World, a national antihunger advocacy group, and Doctors Without Borders.

The most important elements of your visual, or graphic, identity program are your logo (aka "mark") and the logotype that represents your organization's name. Are they distinct, unique and memorable? Are they consistently used in relationship to one another? And are they simple and adaptable to multiple uses? Your graphic identity has to work across all your communications vehicles, everything from invitations and signage to publications and Web use.

> *Are your logo and logotype distinct, unique and memorable?*

Color, secondary typefaces and paper stock are other critical components of your identity and need to be used consistently in all of your materials. Remember, your identity will only be effective if it's used consistently and repeatedly.

Try this exercise to determine how consistent your identity is. Cover up the logo on all of your publications. Would you recognize them as coming from one organization? You should see a consistent use of color, type and images.

It's always helpful to test your identity with sample audiences to help you refine your approach. If your budget permits, conduct professionally administered focus groups with each of your key audiences. Even if you just go to the local shopping center and ask random passersby to react to your potential logos and slogans, the information you gather can be extremely valuable. No matter what method you use, you will be surprised at what you will learn by testing your identity. ■

do-it-yourself guide to re-evaluating your identity

Take out a piece of paper and divide it into four columns:

- In column one, list what your organization does (the services you provide, the audiences you serve) no judgments or adjectives, just the facts about your work.
- In column two, list the words that describe how your organization approaches these issues and serves your constituents. Are you established and collaborative, new and confrontational, multidisciplinary or single-issue focused? List the adjectives that your audiences would use to describe you.
- In column three, translate these adjectives into colors, textures, typefaces and photographic styles. At this stage it might be useful to have samples to look at (design books or even magazines can help) so that you can point to particular shades, fonts or photos that embody your organization's personality.
- In column four, list all of your communications tools – from simple postcards to television public service announcements. Now consider how the list in column three can guide the design of each of your communications vehicles so that all of your materials consistently reflect your image.

creating a style guide

Your messages and communications vehicles should all work together harmoniously to convey a consistent message about your institution. Make sure everyone in your organization knows exactly how to use your logo, colors and other components of your visual identity.

Be sure you have templates, standards and visual/textual style guides to ensure consistency. These should be accessible online so that staff members are not tempted to recreate your logo from scratch if they're in a hurry.

The back pocket of this book contains a sample identity usage guide. Feel free to borrow whatever you need, but it's critical that you have a style guide tailored to your organization's identity.

A style guide or identity manual does not need to be lengthy, but it should include the following:

1. Guidelines for the use of your organization's logo and graphic identity system.
2. Your organization's "house style" relating to capitalization, punctuation, abbreviations and the like.
3. A comprehensive, supplemental reference (such as the *Associated Press Stylebook* or *The Chicago Manual of Style*) and the preferred dictionary for issues not addressed by your in-house style guide.
4. Any variations to your house style for Web and other electronic communications.
5. Naming nomenclature for your key programs, projects and facilities.
6. A glossary of terms specific to your organization or its sphere.
7. Frequently misused or misspelled words.

see sample identity guidelines in the back pocket

roadside assistance

lovemarks: The Future Beyond Brands
by Kevin Roberts (2004)

Idea Index: Graphic Effects and Typographic Treatments
by Jim Krause (2000)

Designing Brand Identity: A Complete Guide to Creating, Building, and Maintaining Strong Brands
by Alina Wheele (2003)

Emotional Branding: The New Paradigm for Connecting Brands to People
by Marc Gobe (2001)

Making and Breaking the Grid: A Graphic Design Layout Workshop
by Timothy Samara (2003)

message development

survey says: MORE THAN 60% OF YOU DO NOT RELY ON AN AGREED-UPON SERIES OF KEY MESSAGES.

WHAT do you want people to know about your organization? When people talk about your nonprofit, what do you want them to say?

Think of the most important points, no more than three, that you want your audience to understand about your organization. These core messages should relate to who you are and why you exist as an organization. For instance, if your mission is to help women with chemical dependencies recover, you may want to emphasize that your services are free, nonjudgmental and confidential.

> Are you inspired and motivated by your own materials?

To make sure your audience begins to embrace your key messages, you need to consistently make the same points in all of your communications and you need to keep your messages simple. To be compelling, your messages must be memorable. Nonprofits frequently make the mistake of devising a dozen complex messages that even their internal audience can't commit to memory. How do you expect those who aren't as close to your organization to remember your messages if those inside aren't able to articulate them easily?

Another test is whether you are inspired and motivated by your own materials. If you don't find your messages compelling, don't expect your audiences to be moved either. You'll want to test your messages on your target audiences to make sure you're hitting the mark.

You may want to develop messages for specific audiences, campaigns, programs and projects. But keep in mind that all messages should relate back to your brand, be memorable and be relevant to your audience. They should include a strong call to action and support your organization's mission. It is also a good idea to develop standard language to describe key programs and projects for use in speeches, letters and proposals; not only does it enhance consistency, but it can save you time.

Once you have developed your messages, you then need to "frame" them so that the individual audiences you want to reach will hear them and listen to them. This means that you might need to change or adjust your messages based on your audience research.

For example, the campaign "Don't Mess With Texas" aimed to reduce the cost of litter removal and keep the state beautiful. The target audience of

15- to 24-year-old males didn't care about either of those goals, so the message was aligned with something that was relevant to them – pride in being a Texan. Similarly, TheTruth.com campaign tapped into the teen psyche by not focusing on the dangers of smoking, but rather on the way the tobacco industry was exploiting the youth market. Instead of it being cool to smoke, it became cool to reject tobacco-industry manipulation.

The "Don't Mess With Texas" and "TheTruth.com" campaigns also are excellent examples of the importance of framing your issue in a way that resonates with the audience you're trying to reach. (Framing is discussed in more detail in Chapter Four, under Advocacy.) ■

eliminating jargon

The Edna McConnell Clark Foundation has developed an online resource to help you eliminate the use of jargon and the confusion it causes. Visit the Jargon Files at www.emcf.org/pub/jargon for a variety of tools to improve your writing, including two book-length essays by Tony Proscio, one of the leading experts in this arena.

storytelling

Nonprofit organizations do important and meaningful work that has the ability to change lives and improve our world. Take the time to harvest the stories that demonstrate the impact your organization has on those it serves. By telling stories of how individuals are affected by the issue you are working to solve, you personalize your mission and goals and make them more memorable.

Storytelling can be used effectively no matter what communications vehicles you employ — from your annual report and case for support to your Web site and direct-mail appeals. The best stories have a beginning, middle and end; establish the heroes and villains; involve a conflict; and have an emotional hook.

seven questions to sharpen your stories

- Who's the protagonist?
- What keeps it interesting?
- Have you included telling details?
- Is the meaning clear?
- What's the hook?
- Where's the conflict?
- What's the emotional hook?

Source: Andy Goodman, Storytelling as Best Practice

messages that stick

The most effective and memorable messages are:

- Simple, making use of analogies. (The Center for Science in the Public Interest, for example, refers to fettuccine alfredo as "a heart attack on a plate.")
- Unexpected, producing a short circuit between two mental frames. (The Ad Council's "buckle up" commercial pretends to be an ad for a new family minivan, until the van is struck broadside by another car.)
- Concrete, using specific language and details.
- Credentialed, relying on authorities or testable ideas.
- Emotional, tapping negative or positive feelings.
- Stories with real people. (Subway's advertisements with weight-loss hero Jared Fogel worked better than "six sandwiches under six grams of fat.")

Source: "Loud and Clear: Crafting Messages That Stick – What Nonprofits Can Learn From Urban Legend," by Chip Heath, in Stanford Social Innovation Review

roadside assistance

www.frameworksinstitute.org
Frameworks Institute's Web site includes ideas for framing your messages for greater impact.

The Springboard: How Storytelling Ignites Action in Knowledge-Era Organizations
by Stephen Denning (2000)

Storytelling in Organizations: How Narrative and Storytelling Are Transforming 21st Century Management
by John Seely Brown, Steve Denning, Katalina Groh and Larry Prusak (2004)

Storytelling for Grantseekers: Telling Your Organization's Story
by Cheryl Clarke (2001)

TOP TIPS

- Develop a strategic communications plan with specific, measurable and realistic goals.

- Plan for potential crises so that negative impact is minimized.

- Build your brand by distinguishing your organization from other institutions.

- Your organizational identity is a key component of your brand. Develop it strategically and protect it vigorously.

- Frame your messages to ensure relevance to your audiences and make sure your messages are memorable.

- Use storytelling as a technique to inspire your audiences and personalize your organization's messages.

chapter three
how do we get there?

Knowing where you want to go is not enough to get you to your destination. You need financial and human resources to drive your communications program. It's not hard to find support for the concept of improving your organization's communications efforts, but when it comes down to allocating the necessary people power and funds, it can be more challenging.

How can you secure sufficient funding to implement your plan when your nonprofit has so many other pressing needs competing for limited resources? And how can you ensure that the time and money you'll spend on your communications efforts will not only be effective, but also will be valued by the organization?

In this chapter, we'll discuss the nuts and bolts of assembling your budget, selling your plan to your board, finding funds when resources are scarce, hiring staff or a consultant, and collaborating with like-minded organizations for cost-sharing and greater impact.

creating a budget

survey says: 60% OF YOU SPEND LESS THAN 1% OF YOUR TOTAL BUDGET ON COMMUNICATIONS.

CHANCES ARE your budget isn't as large as you'd like it to be, which means that creating a realistic and carefully crafted budget is even more important to keeping your program on track.

The process of assigning actual dollar amounts to particular projects can be a real eye-opener, but it also can be used as a buy-in tool with your board to demonstrate the investment that is necessary to implement your plan.

For each component of your communications program, you need to develop an outline, sometimes referred to as a project brief, that succinctly describes the project, its purpose and expected outcomes, its timeline and an itemized list of the costs involved. Be realistic about what things actually cost and how long they take to complete. A change in the timeline can have a significant impact on the budget. For instance, you can incur rush fees for print and design if a publication you initially planned on doing four months down the road suddenly needs to be produced in three weeks, or if your event is moved up from August to April.

Once you've listed each project and all of the associated line-item costs, you'll probably find that your planned expenses exceed your available funding. Now comes the difficult part of determining what pieces and projects can be eliminated or delayed until the next budget cycle, and which are essential to your program.

It pays to be a bit conservative in your estimates so you'll be prepared if something changes down the road. Adding a line item for unanticipated expenses, or a small cushion on the budget for a major project, can mean you won't have to scrap your newsletter at the last minute if the cost of paper or postage goes up unexpectedly in the third quarter of your budget year.

And remember that the best way to build a bigger budget is to demonstrate that the funds you've spent have shown a return on investment. The more you can show how well it's working, either through surveys of happy audiences or, better yet, with additional funds that further your organization's mission, the bigger your communications budget will grow over time. ■

stretching limited dollars

Following are a few ideas for using your communications funds wisely:

- When resources are limited, it's even more important that you reach the right audience with the right message. One of the best investments you can make is to research your audience before investing in any communications vehicle. Remember, research doesn't have to be expensive. See Chapter One, Research Basics, for low-cost research strategies.
- Take advantage of the latest electronic communications tools. In March 2004, the *Wall Street Journal* reported on a McKinsey & Co. study that showed online solicitations cost only 20 cents compared with $1 or more for direct-mail and telephone solicitations. See Web Sites and Media, both in Chapter Four, for several cost-saving ideas.
- With your publications, it can be relatively easy to save costs without sacrificing quality by making a few minor adjustments in your print specifications. If funding is tight, you might reduce the number of pages of your newsletter from eight to six, or even four. A simple change in paper stock can have an enormous impact on the bottom line. See Chapter Four, Marketing Materials, for more suggestions.

budget checklist

Following are a few details to consider as you put your budget together:

- Know the cost per piece of the materials you produce. However, don't make your decisions based on cost alone. Sometimes a higher cost per piece will also have a correspondingly higher level of readership.
- Get competitive bids for every project. Ask for bids offering the same level of quality.
- Check credentials and client references, as well as portfolios and other work samples. Know exactly what you're getting for your money.
- Don't forget the small details. Design, print and photography estimates often do not include sales tax.
- Check to make sure your images are royalty-free, or that you've negotiated the usage rights that you need. (See Marketing Materials in Chapter Four for more information.)

roadside assistance

The Budget-Building Book for Nonprofits: A Step-By-Step Guide for Managers and Boards
by Murray Dropkin and
Bill LaTouche (1998)

*Budgeting for
Not-For-Profit Organizations*
by David Maddox (1999)

*Handbook of Budgeting for
Nonprofit Organizations*
by Jae K. Shim, et al. (1996)

finding funds

survey says: 71% OF YOU DESCRIBED YOUR COMMUNICATIONS BUDGET AS "NO BUDGET" OR "COULD BE BETTER."

so how do you build a comprehensive communications program when your plans are big but your budget isn't? You have more options than are obvious.

Consider asking an individual donor to underwrite the cost of a particular publication or communications project. This is an often-overlooked strategy that can strengthen your organization's relationship with a donor while attracting additional supporters through the new communications piece.

> You're not alone! The key to finding funds is to be creative, and don't be afraid to ask.

Relying on volunteers (such as retired executives and reporters) and obtaining pro-bono assistance from lawyers and accountants can also can help you stretch your limited resources further.

Pro-bono services can be a tremendous resource if handled professionally. If you accept favors or freebies, however, be sure to follow normal business protocols by clearly outlining project details and expectations and obtaining signed contracts. Identify the value of the services, even if it's a trade.

Corporate sponsors may also be available, either as funders or for in-kind donations (such as wine for an event or computers and software from technology companies).

And the foundation world is also aware of the power of communications and is increasingly funding communications initiatives.

You're not alone. The key to finding funds is to be creative. Don't be afraid to ask. And be tenacious. Remember the sales caveat that 9 percent of the salespeople make 90 percent of the sales because they don't give up. ■

add communications to all grant requests

More and more foundations see the wisdom of funding a communications component in the grants they give. They're doing this because they see how communications can:

- Raise awareness of causes they support and people they want to help
- Move an organization to greater levels of self-sufficiency – reaching new donors and people in the community who then lend their support

Remember to educate your board about the staff resources you need to support the programs you want to fund. Funding for communications should be a key component in all grant requests.

> Build a budget for communications. Maybe you won't get 5 percent of your organization's total budget, but organizations need to start budgeting for communications the same way they include payroll and rent. Start small and build on your successes.

find corporate partners

Creative cause-marketing partnerships can generate significant budget dollars for nonprofits. The United States Fund for Unicef expects to raise $4 million to $5 million per year through events and sales of reproductions of the giant Baccarat-crystal snowflake that adorns the intersection of 57th Street and 5th Avenue in New York City, according to a November 2004 article in *The New York Times*. Many corporations look for opportunities in the nonprofit sector. Think creatively about who is likely to help and who fits with your organization.

identify 'friends'

In the communications field, it's easy to find a sympathetic ear. Agency principals, freelancers and even marketing departments of big companies are all likely prospects to volunteer services. These are people who know the difference communications can make, since it's their chosen profession. They're one of your best groups of allies.

selling It

survey says: 80% OF YOU SAY YOUR BOARD DISCUSSES COMMUNICATIONS ONCE A YEAR OR LESS.

WHAT IF your organization believes it values communications but acts otherwise? If you don't have the support you need, your journey may be over before it's even begun.

Does your nonprofit allocate a set percentage of the organization's overall budget to communications? Or do you have to demonstrate the need for communications funding year after year? Maybe your board or senior administration is worried that some constituents will view an aggressive communications effort as a waste of budget. Or they like your ideas but water them down through a bureaucratic process.

> In the modern world of business, it is useless to be a creative original thinker unless you can also **SELL** what you create. Management cannot be expected to recognize a good idea unless it is presented to them by a good [salesperson].
> — advertising mogul david m. ogilvy

Remember to use communications as the business tool that it is. Nonprofit boards often include successful business leaders. Measure the return on investment and the projected results of your efforts in language your board understands — the financial impact.

Show the return on investment that might be gained through a direct-mail effort or a media relations program. If you've done a competitive analysis, show the board what the other organizations in your community — those who are trying to get attention from the same audiences you want to reach — are doing.

Have a problem with general awareness? Take a video camera (and release forms) to a shopping mall and ask passersby what they know about your organization/issue. Your board may be more willing to consider an increased investment in communications when faced with the reality that the messages they think are clear and convincing are not getting through to your audience.

The planning phase of a major capital campaign for your organization is a great opportunity to leverage increased funding for your ongoing communications efforts. It's easier for the board to understand the need for investment when a campaign is being considered, and a strong reputation among key constituents is a prerequisite to a successful fundraising campaign.

Don't forget that you also need to sell your communications plan to employees, volunteers and other key influencers throughout the organization. If your staff doesn't speak with one voice externally, your organization will be sending an inconsistent message that can undermine your efforts.

And don't let your board or senior team become backseat drivers. Prohibit design, or crafting of communications projects, by committee. Protect the creative process and put clear limits on the review-and-approval process. ■

watch your language

Board members and colleagues in non-communications functions often find our tools of trade perplexing, and they may be uncomfortable with their own lack of technical understanding. Whether you're talking about media buys, PMS colors, search engine optimization or why you can't add just one more page to a publication, you're often perceived as speaking a foreign language. Take the time to educate your senior team and avoid jargon whenever possible. Speak the board's language – talk about how communications can help them achieve their objectives.

"It is often the case that nonprofit organizations want communications to be easy. Ironically, they want sound-bite answers to the same social problems whose complexity they understand all too well. While policy research and formulation are given their due as tough, demanding areas of an organization's work plan, communications is seen as 'soft.' While program development and practice are seen as requiring expertise and the thoughtful consideration of best practices, communications is an 'anyone can do it if you have to' task. It is time to retire this thinking. Doing communications strategically requires the same investment of intellect and study that these other areas of nonprofit practice have been accorded." Frameworks Institute

http://frameworksinstitute.org/strategicanalysis/perspective.shtml

see photo/video release form in the back pocket

roadside assistance

The Nonprofit Leadership Team
by Fisher Howe (2003)

Nonprofit Board Answer Book
by Robert C. Andringa and
Ted W. Engstrom (1998)

www.boardcafe.org
(electronic newsletter for
nonprofit boards)

Frameworks
www.frameworksinstitute.org

hiring help: staff or consultant?

survey says: MORE THAN 50% OF YOU HIRE WITHOUT FIRST CREATING A JOB DESCRIPTION.

IN THE nonprofit world, where staff members wear a variety of hats and are always spread too thin, it's unlikely you'll be able to hire as many people as you could put to good use. You'll have to prioritize what to handle in-house, what can be done by a consultant, and what will have to remain undone until additional budget or staff becomes available. For most nonprofits, it's always preferable to have someone inside the organization focusing exclusively on communications issues, but it's a luxury some institutions cannot afford.

For many projects, especially audits and surveys, consultants can save you money in the long run and help you make a stronger case with your board. Their experience implementing best practices at a variety of institutions – and sometimes their outsider status – often give their opinions greater weight than those of in-house staff. Key audiences and senior leadership may be more candid with a consultant, providing more valuable feedback. And a consultant may help facilitate consensus more readily than an internal communications expert.

Break down the type of assistance you require. Do you need a senior-level expert for 25 percent of the work, clerical help for another 25 percent, and writing/editing support for the balance of the project? If so, hiring a consultant can provide more cost-effective support than a full-time staff member hired at too high or too low a level for the work you need to accomplish.

Of course, you'll need to evaluate your organization's unique situation to make an informed decision about whether to stay in-house or use a consultant. When a new executive director or communications director is hired, for instance, that person can bring a fresh perspective and an outsider's objectivity. Or your budget may be so tight that hiring a consultant is out of the question. It's even more important under those circumstances to build the case with your board about the return on investment in communications. Is the budget really that limited or does the board lack belief in the value of marketing? ∎

hiring help

Once you know your top communications needs, think about who can best fill them.

- Is your need media relations, publications or marketing? Perhaps you need a senior communications specialist who has experience in a wide range of disciplines.
- Hire someone who complements your current team and fills in gaps of experience and skills.
- If you can hire only one communications staff member, develop a realistic job description. It's hard to find a person who can meet all your needs.
- Check references and give a skills test that speaks to the work you need to have done.
- Don't be afraid to ask the obvious. If you hired a PC-only person for a Mac-based environment, there's a steep learning curve for both you and them.

six good reasons to hire a consultant

1. No one in-house has the expertise you need.
2. You have the know-how but not the time.
3. You're too close to the issue and can't be impartial.
4. The project is confidential and inappropriate to assign internally.
5. You need an expert's credentials to help you sell your board.
6. You need help on several levels, so it's not cost-effective to hire a single person.

tips for working with consultants

- Choose the right consultant for the right project. Is it a good fit? Do they have a track record of success with the type of issues you are facing? Shop around.
- Check references. Does the consultant consistently deliver on time and on budget? Take a look at the consultant's previous work.
- Ensure you are on the same page regarding the creative and budgetary aspects of the project.
- Clearly delineate roles, responsibilities, processes, payment terms and timeline.
- Remember, a consultant can sometimes feel threatening to in-house staff. Seek buy-in from the staff and explain what you hope to accomplish with outside help.
- Be clear about who will oversee the work and serve as the key contact. Does this person have the authority to make critical decisions? If not, you're setting yourself up for multiple revisions and/or work that upper management may not approve.
- Do the prep work necessary to bring the consultant up to speed (e.g., gathering facts and figures, providing an exact scope of services).
- Put your agreement in writing and include a clause that allows you to gracefully – and legally – bow out for any reason, incurring only the costs of work actually undertaken. Remember, verbal agreements are binding contracts in many states.
- Don't second-guess your consultants. You've hired them for a reason and, if you've made a good hire and effectively communicated your goals, trust their professional advice.
- Don't expect the consultant to be solely responsible for developing your plan or establishing your mission, vision and goals. The consultant's role is to facilitate your decision-making process, not to determine strategic direction.

One of the best ways to ensure your projects stay on track and on budget is to have your consultant produce a creative brief outlining agreed-upon goals, timeline and other critical elements.

see sample creative brief in the back pocket

no one can do it all

No one person can realistically handle all needs. Create a job description that speaks to your most strategic communications needs. Such clarity of focus will yield greater success and increase the likelihood you'll be able to hire additional help down the road.

roadside assistance

www.nptimes.com
(The NonProfit Times publishes an annual salary survey in its February issue)

www.guidestar.org
(in-depth nonprofit salary information)

www.jobstar.com
(listing of salary surveys, including a section on nonprofits)

www.salary.com
(includes a nonprofit section and geographic-specific information)

www.salarysource.com
(tracks salaries for 350 position titles, although mostly for the corporate sector; it includes a large number of communications titles)

collaborating

survey says: FEW OF YOU HAVE PARTNERED WITH OTHER ORGANIZATIONS ON COMMUNICATIONS.

WHAT IF similar organizations, with similar communications goals, worked together to inform audiences about important calls to action, such as increasing voter registration or stopping domestic violence? Such collaboration can enhance media coverage, build widespread support for your common objective and avoid duplication of effort.

Who is doing the same sort of work, or complementary work, and how can you collaborate to mobilize efforts, save money and have a greater impact? Whether you partner with other nonprofits, like-minded service providers, corporate sponsors, foundations, universities, government agencies or the media, opportunities for meaningful strategic alliances are plentiful.

> Such collaboration can build widespread support for your common objective.

You may be able to attract more media coverage for your report on environmental pollutants by building a coalition of health agencies, environmental groups and neighborhood associations. A coalition of theater companies might want to jointly advertise their upcoming performances to save money.

Nonprofit coalitions can leverage significant increases in funding for collaborative communications efforts. Savvy donors want their dollars to have the biggest impact possible. Like-minded institutions partnering to reduce overlap and increase the reach of their messages will find donors ready to join their cause. Such practices also make nonprofits more accountable to donors and allow them to more effectively serve their audiences.

"One way to increase the already formidable impact of the nonprofit sector is to increase the efficiency of the dollars we raise and spend," wrote Patrick Foye, president and CEO of United Way of Long Island, in a recent editorial in *The New York Times*. "This can be done by making the most of technology to reduce operating and fundraising costs, by joining with other agencies to avoid duplication, by taking advantage of volume purchasing and by working with our federal, state and local government partners to maximize the returns." ■

evaluating potential partners

Here are seven questions you should ask before collaborating with an external partner:

1. Are your organizations' cultures, values and ethics compatible?
2. Does the other organization have a clear mission and strategic plan? Is the organization well-managed?
3. What can they bring to the table? Why does it benefit you to partner?
4. Would you have stronger capacity to serve constituents by working together than you would separately?
5. Does your leadership support the collaboration? Does theirs?
6. Who are their other partners?
7. Do you have a written agreement that details the objectives and goals of your collaboration, outlines expectations and allows you to back out if necessary?

cause-related marketing

Corporations increasingly are recognizing the value of strategic alliances with the nonprofit sector. In 2004, corporate spending on cause marketing approached $1 billion, according to a recent report by PowerPact, LLC and Cause Marketing Forum, the results of which were published in *PR Newswire*.

"A novel concept only 20 years ago, cause marketing is now a core strategy for many companies in the post-9/11, post-Enron period," says David Hessekiel, Cause Marketing Forum president. "This study indicates that cause marketing's growth will accelerate as manufacturers and retailers learn to better integrate their efforts."

Alison Glander, CEO of PowerPact, adds: "Generating consumer dollars for cause programs also builds awareness of social issues and develops loyal constituencies for nonprofits. The people who are shopping with a cause in mind are the same people who will get out and lobby."

A 2003 survey found that 71 percent of consumers are more likely to buy a product if it helps a charity. And although the amount of royalty revenues generated by nonprofit deals pales in comparison with that of corporate licensing, $39 million compared with $5.8 billion in 2002, nonprofit licensing grew by 25 percent between 1999 and 2002, according to a June 2004 story in *On Philanthropy*.

One example is the partnership between the National Wildlife Federation and Home Depot to create products for their "Backyard Wildlife Sanctuary" initiative, which featured such items as bird seed and birdfeeders.

The Independent Sector Web site features a host of stories about corporate/nonprofit partnerships, including Girls Inc. and cosmetics company Lancome's alliance to help empower girls, and Starbucks and America SCORES' collaboration to create a safe environment for children after school.

media sponsorships

A number of media outlets sponsor charitable causes, especially if the charity holds large events through which the publication, radio or TV station can build brand awareness and loyalty. For example, in exchange for having its logo included on the nonprofit's marketing items (T-shirts, brochures, posters, banners, ads, etc.), a newspaper may offer the charity free advertising space. A radio or television station may offer a deejay or anchor to serve as emcee for the event. Some media outlets even donate money.

roadside assistance

The Collaboration Challenge: How Nonprofits and Businesses Succeed Through Strategic Alliances
by James E. Austin (2000)

Making Money While Making a Difference: How to Profit with a Nonprofit Partner
by Richard Steckel et al. (1999)

www.independentsector.org/mission_market
Resource Center for Effective Corporate-Nonprofit Partnerships

The Art of Cause Marketing
by Richard Earle (2000)

TOP TIPS

- Clearly outline costs and expectations in your budget.

- Be realistic about what things actually cost.

- Identify specifics about the areas and levels of expertise you are missing before hiring staff or consultants.

- Clearly delineate expectations and timeframe to your consultants and get everything in writing.

- Partner with like-minded organizations to maximize the effectiveness of your communications and expand your reach.

- Show your board members the return they'll receive from investing in communications, whether increasing revenues, advancing mission or building reputation.

chapter four
what to take

You've done the hard work of figuring out where you are as an organization, where you want to go and the resources you need to get there. Now it's time to choose the right combination of tools to implement your communications plan effectively.

With such a wide range of options available, from print publications and Web sites to direct mail and media relations, how do you know which are best for your organization and its goals? You'll want to look at cost, of course, but also the appropriateness of each option for reaching your specific audience.

This chapter goes into detail about tried-and-true, as well as innovative and new, communications tools and how to put together the right mix to meet the needs of your nonprofit.

advertising

survey says: 18% OF YOU CURRENTLY USE ADVERTISING AS PART OF YOUR COMMUNICATIONS EFFORT.

WHILE ADVERTISING is one of the most visible communications tools available, it might be the one that you use the least. Advertising allows you to maintain complete control over content, but it requires a significant budget and long-term commitment to be the most effective.

The following attributes are vital to any advertising strategy:

Reach The number of people in your target audience who will see, hear or read your advertisement is referred to as "reach."

Frequency No matter how strong your message, people need to hear your message repeatedly for it to sink in. Keep in mind that by the time you and your board are sick of a message, it's probably only starting to resonate with your audience.

Memorability Make certain your message is memorable. In advertising, you have only a moment to make an impact. Your audience won't act on your ad if they don't remember it.

Appropriateness The vehicles for your ads must be appropriate for your objective and for your target audience. For instance, you wouldn't advertise in *The New York Times* to invite donors to an event. Ads for your cause don't need to reach the widest possible audience to be effective; they just need to reach the right audience.

Also consider ethnic media in your planning. According to a report by New California Media, "Forty percent [of ethnic Californians] say they pay more attention to television, radio and newspaper ads in the language of their home country than to English-language ads." ■

> Half of the money I spend on advertising is **WASTED**; the trouble is I don't know which half.
> department store pioneer
> john wanamaker

public service announcements

Newspapers and television and radio stations receive hundreds of public service announcements each year. PSAs can be a great way of combining free placement with a controlled message, but you will have little influence over when, or if, your ad is used.

With print and television ads, you have to pay for production costs – unless you can get them donated. Radio spots can be very inexpensive, especially if read by an announcer who works at the station.

To increase the chances of your PSA being used, be sure that your print ads are standard size (check with your target newspapers and magazines) and that broadcast ads are the right format and length (generally 15-second, 30-second or one-minute spots). Keep in mind that the higher the quality of the message and visuals, the more likely your PSA will run. And it's almost always worth a call to see if you can get individual stations to agree to run your spots at specific times.

"From time to time, some organizations decide to make an investment in paid campaigns to complement their public service campaigns," said Peggy Conlon, president and chief executive at the Advertising Council in New York. "It's a perfectly good strategy, but year after year, the donated-media, public-service-advertising model really is the best for nonprofits."

paying to be heard

Many nonprofits are starting to emulate the corporate sector in order to get their messages noticed amid all the information clutter.

The New York Times recently reported on the American Heart Association's $36 million, three-year campaign that it launched early in 2004, the first such effort in its history.

"It's been common for charities to get donated advertising," said Stephen M. Adler, chief executive at JAMI Charity Brands in New York, which helps match nonprofit groups with corporate benefactors. "But what's happening now is charities are having a harder time reaching their target audiences."

"Increasingly, nonprofits are getting more sophisticated," Candy Cox, managing partner of DDB Worldwide, told *The Times*. "They want to play in the very best media in order to communicate their messages."

online advertising

A surge in online advertising is being led by paid-for text-links or by search engines such as Google and Yahoo! The response rate from people clicking on paid links can be as low as 1 percent, about the same as direct mail. But there is an important [plus]: Internet advertisers usually pay only if someone clicks on their link. This is the equivalent of paying for the delivery of junk mail only to households that read it.

Source: The Economist, *June 2004*

> Online advertising [is] growing twice as fast as cable TV advertising and more than three times faster than advertising in any other medium, according to a study by Jupiter Research.
>
> *Source: Ad Age.com, July 2004*

roadside assistance

Advertising Council
www.adcouncil.org

PSA Research Center at
Goodwill Communications
www.psaresearch.com

American Association of
Advertising Agencies
www.aaaa.org

Advertopedia
www.advertopedia.com

advocacy

survey says: 39% OF YOU RATE POLITICAL OUTREACH AND ADVOCACY AS KEY COMPONENTS OF YOUR COMMUNICATIONS EFFORTS.

SHAPING public opinion about your cause and influencing legislation remain among the most challenging tasks facing nonprofit organizations. Legislation and court decisions relating to health care, welfare, the environment, minimum wage, human rights, and a thousand other topics, profoundly affect nonprofit organizations and the type of charitable services that society needs.

Depending on the scope of your issue, it may be important for you to reach out to elected officials locally, regionally and nationally. Keep policymakers informed about your organization and aware of the key issues facing your communities. Determine which of their aides handles the issues that are important to your cause, and then make them aware of the relevant facts and figures from your perspective.

> Your aim is to get your cause on the public agenda, and shape the way your issue is covered in the media.

Learn when government agencies and legislators are going to discuss and act upon issues of importance to your constituents. If you have a compelling story, try to arrange meetings with everyone from your local city council members all the way to top state and national officials. Make sure they know how many people your organization can reach. Build understanding and awareness of your concerns by using moments of interaction with policymakers and their staffs as "teachable" moments rather than as debates.

Your advocacy efforts also should extend to the news media, which can play a vital role in educating both the general population and those you serve about your issues. You should aim not only to get your cause on the public agenda, but also to shift the way stories on your issue are reported in the media. The way a reporter frames a story can significantly affect public perception of your issue.

Is the reporter emphasizing the public policy issues surrounding stories about urban blight, child endangerment or animal rights? Or do the stories focus narrowly on the specific individuals involved? If it's the latter, your message can easily get lost. In a comprehensive study of 10,000 local and national television news reports on international events and issues, the Center for Media and Public Affairs found that less than 1 percent focused on the big-picture, public policy issues that can effect societal change. Motivate your constituents to write letters to the op-ed section of various media to help drive home your points and reframe the issue.

Web sites and guerilla marketing play an increasingly important role in advocacy campaigns. Many nonprofits, including the American Cancer Society, have a "talk with your legislator" button on their Web sites. An e-mail alert can reach thousands quickly and economically. And those who become committed to your cause are likely to help spread the word through viral marketing – passing your message on to their friends and family.

Another good tool for generating buzz is releasing the results of a study or issuing a report card on an industry. This gives you a news hook and an opportunity to translate complicated issues into quantifiable information. Tapping into what's currently happening in popular culture also can help make your issue more appealing to the media.

five essential steps in an advocacy campaign

1. Determine your goals.
2. Identify and segment your audiences and understand their current perceptions.
3. Craft compelling messages.
4. Determine the appropriate vehicles and best spokespeople to reach each audience.
5. Spell out the actions you want people to take.

writing letters

Whether you want to mobilize constituents to write to their congressmen or draft opinion letters to your local newspaper, follow these simple steps to quickly build momentum for your cause:

- Draft a few sentences or key points about the message you want your constituents to convey to decision-makers or the media.
- Develop a "contact tree" to carry your key messages and the goal of the letter-writing campaign to all appropriate constituents. Call the first two people on your tree, who then begin circulating your key points and target audience (legislative or media) to two or three others, who each contact two or three others each, and so on.
- Encourage participants to stay on point but to personalize their letters so they don't look like spam.

calling legislators

Help your constituents advocate for your cause by making it easy for them to get in touch with their legislators. Include contact information in your mailings and other advocacy efforts. Go to www.congress.org for contact information on the president, vice president, U.S. Congress, and state and local officials. The site also contains a media guide to find information for national and local editors and reporters.

roadside assistance

The Alliance for Justice (866.NPLOBBY/ www.allianceforjustice.org) offers technical assistance on what election activities nonprofits can and cannot do.

Loud and Clear in an Election Year: Amplifying the Voices of Community Advocates edited by Holly Minch (2004)

Frameworks Institute www.frameworksinstitute.org

Fact Check – a nonpartisan "consumer advocate" that aims to reduce the level of deception and confusion in U.S. politics, from the Annenberg Public Policy Center of the University of Pennsylvania www.factcheck.org

Making the News: A Guide for Nonprofits and Activists by Jason Salzman (1998)

capital campaigns

survey says: THE MAJORITY OF YOU WHO ARE CONDUCTING CAPITAL CAMPAIGNS HAVE NEVER WORKED ON ONE PREVIOUSLY.

UNIVERSITIES AND LARGE NONPROFITS have perfected the capital campaign as a strategy for raising a significant sum of money above and beyond normal fundraising efforts in a limited period of time. The specific timeframe and goals motivate donors to make "stretch" gifts, larger than what they might normally consider. And campaigns can be effective for all sizes of nonprofits.

If you decide to embark on a campaign, you'll need to make an investment in communicating to major donors and prospective donors (aka prospects), key volunteers, staff and the media, as well as community and often national decision-makers. Keep in mind that the majority of funding will come from a small number of supporters. The standard rule is that 80 percent of your gifts will be made by 20 percent of donors.

To understand what will motivate that select but crucial audience, it is essential that you conduct a feasibility study before launching a campaign. Typically, external fundraising counsel conducts this in-depth assessment of an institution's readiness and fundraising potential. The feasibility study will help determine and test your campaign's financial goal, priorities and key messages.

Prospect research can help you identify new major donors and help target your solicitations to increase the likelihood of success. Such research is invaluable as you tailor fundraising proposals and campaign publications.

The case for support, sometimes called a "case statement," is the fundamental blueprint for marketing your campaign. It literally "makes the case" for why donors should support your campaign. The process of developing your written case also helps build consensus internally on the campaign's priority projects, key messages and ultimate goals – financially and institutionally.

And remember that publicity too early in your campaign can undermine your progress. Don't officially announce your campaign effort until at least one-third to one-half of your financial goal has been pledged by donors.

ask your donors

Conducting focus groups of prospective donors can provide you with valuable feedback for your case statement while also achieving buy-in for the concept of your campaign and its priorities. Donors can tell you directly what would sell them on the campaign, and that's a great cultivation tool as well as a means of targeting and fine-tuning your communications.

producing an effective case statement

- Make a compelling case for why your organization is a smart investment. How will donor funds be used? What meaningful difference will donor gifts make?
- Think big. What significant societal issues will donor support help influence? Why is your organization uniquely qualified to successfully address those issues?
- Aim to win both hearts and minds. Evoke an emotional response in your reader, but provide logical rationale for supporting your institution as well.
- Include a call to action. To be effective, a case statement should have a sense of urgency. Why is donor support needed now?
- Avoid hyperbole. By all means, make bold statements about your institution's strengths and vision, but back up your claims with evidence.
- Demonstrate existing support for your institution by featuring testimonials from constituents and other donors, and/or by listing your board of trustees and campaign leadership, particularly if they are well-known and respected in your community.
- Focus on what might motivate a donor to give, not on your organization's needs.
- Write concisely, memorably and clearly.
- Make sure your printed case is visually appealing. Invest the necessary resources for photography, design and printing. The case for support does not have to be expensive, but it must reinforce your point that the campaign is a smart investment. See Marketing Materials in this chapter for tips on saving money on publications without sacrificing quality.
- The format of your case for support must be customized to suit your institution's personality, history, mission, campaign goals and the donors you aim to reach.
- It's often a good idea to include a list of giving opportunities, large and small, to motivate donors and show specifically where they might make an investment.

feasibility-study topics

Following are the key areas that should be discussed with interviewees in a capital campaign feasibility study, according to the Center on Philanthropy at Indiana University:

- Case (why should donors support the campaign?)
- Proposed goal (what dollar amount should be the campaign goal?)
- Leadership (who would be the right volunteer leader of the campaign?)
- Gift potential (how much would the interviewee consider giving to such a campaign?)
- Timing (when should the campaign be launched and how long should it last?)
- Public relations (what public relations efforts should be included in the campaign?)
- Referrals for other interviews (who else should be interviewed for the feasibility study?)
- Special areas of concern (what other factors does the interviewee think would influence the success of the campaign or his/her own participation?)

key campaign communication vehicles

- Case for support
- Newsletter
- Video/DVD
- Web site
- Brochures on planned giving, endowment, featured priorities, etc.
- Graphic-identity program (logo and other visuals) specific to campaign
- Press releases about major gifts
- Campaign press kit and fact sheets
- Events (campaign kickoff and completion celebration)
- Scripted remarks

roadside assistance

www.philanthropy.iupui.edu
The Center on Philanthropy at Indiana University and its Fund Raising School offer myriad courses and tools to help you successfully launch a capital campaign.

www.philanthropy.com
The Chronicle of Philanthropy routinely reports on fundraising campaigns at large and small institutions across the country.

Conducting a Successful Capital Campaign: The New, Revised and Expanded Edition of the Leading Guide to Planning and Implementing a Capital Campaign
by Kent E. Dove (1999)

Preparing Your Capital Campaign: An Excellence in Fund Raising Workbook Series publication
by Marilyn Bancel (2000)

www.onphilanthropy.com

direct mail

survey says: HALF OF YOU RATE DIRECT MAIL AS AN IMPORTANT PART OF YOUR COMMUNICATIONS EFFORT, YET LESS THAN 5% MEASURE ITS EFFECTIVENESS.

DIRECT MAIL is the staple of most nonprofit fundraising operations. It is used primarily to acquire new donors, renew and upgrade existing donors, and identify planned-giving prospects. It is also effective for special efforts, i.e., to raise funds for specific programs or projects over and above your annual appeal to donors. Direct mail puts your targeted message directly into the hands of your audience, reminding them that you need their continued support.

In addition to its importance as a fundraising vehicle, direct mail can help you build awareness through informational mailings about your organization; it can drive traffic to your Web site; inform constituents of new services; educate your audience about current issues; and much more.

According to Grizzard Communications, an 84-year-old firm that specializes in direct-mail fundraising, 40 percent of your direct-mail success depends on how well you know your audience; 40 percent depends on what you say to them; and the remaining 20 percent depends on how your mailing looks.

> Direct mail puts your targeted message directly into the hands of your audience.

The research you did as suggested in Chapter One will help you address the first point.

For the second issue, it's important to keep in mind why people make philanthropic gifts. Grizzard boils it down to these five reasons: "kindness, a sense of altruism toward others; conscience, the desire to make our world a better place; tenderness, empathy with the poor and disadvantaged; obligation, the perceived duty to share one's abundance; and personal gratification, a sense of 'feeling good' because they have done something significant to help others." Your appeal should evoke an emotional response in your readers, with a hook that moves them to immediate action.

To make your direct-mail piece inviting, so that donors open and act upon, rather than discard, your appeal, it's important to test your design with a small segment of your audience before mailing to large numbers. Testing various strategies will help you determine which appeal will be most effective. Keep your approach interesting to get your mailing opened and read amid all the competing information your audience receives, but don't sacrifice consistency. Use related visuals to build your brand equity and reinforce your message in your donors' minds. ■

attracting planned gifts

Direct mail is an excellent venue for educating your constituents about the benefits of making a planned gift to your organization. Planned gifts make it possible for many donors to have a larger impact philanthropically than they could otherwise afford. And because planned gifts typically offer significant benefits to both the nonprofit and the donor, such as lifetime income and a variety of tax savings, response to direct mail on the subject is generally strong.

You might want to consider mailing a brochure on planned giving in general – or on specific areas such as charitable gift annuities or bequests. Other options include adding a column on planned giving to your donor newsletter, sending out a postcard directing donors to a planned-giving Web site, or writing a targeted appeal letter to all donors and prospects 60 and older.

timing your solicitation

For most organizations and communities, it pays not to mail during the summer, one month prior to an election, or just before the end of the calendar year, when your audience may be overwhelmed with holiday preparations and mail.

maintaining an accurate database

Your database can be your biggest headache or your greatest resource. It's crucial to accurately compile and update your donor names, addresses, salutations, e-mail addresses and other vital information. You can capture details on prospective donors by making "for more information" cards available at your events and in your facilities.

Your database also should include the amount and dates of gifts, what events donors have attended, what mailings they have received, corporate-matching gift programs, and whether any outstanding pledge payments remain and when they are due. By getting the basics down, you reassure donors that your organization is professionally run and that you care about them. If donors have to keep reminding you that they moved three years ago or that they've already completed a pledge, their confidence in your nonprofit may be eroded.

A variety of database software packages and services are on the market, many of which are tailored for nonprofits. Ask peers and colleagues what type of program they use and what their experience has been with the software. Shop around. Take time to evaluate the kind of information you need to track for your nonprofit and choose the software that best fits your specific needs.

roadside assistance

Building Your Direct Mail Program by Gwyneth J. Lister (2001)

www.nonprofitmailers.org
The Alliance of Nonprofit Mailers is a national coalition of nonprofit organizations that uses the mails to raise funds, solicit members and disseminate information. Its site includes a wide range of tools and information, including postal regulations.

www.dmnews.com
DM News dubs itself "the online newspaper of record for direct marketers."

www.the-dma.org
The Direct Marketing Association's site includes industry news, upcoming events and marketing tips.

www.usps.com
The official site of the U.S. Postal Service

donor cultivation and grant writing

survey says: WHILE MANY OF YOU ARE ASKED TO WRITE GRANTS, VERY FEW OF YOU ARE EXPERIENCED GRANT WRITERS.

IN ORDER TO obtain major gifts, you need to master the art of donor cultivation and targeted proposal writing. Your existing donors need to feel appreciated for their support in order to consider making another gift to your institution. And for all major-gift prospects, you need to effectively express a compelling reason why your nonprofit is worthy of their support.

Many nonprofits focus their grant-writing efforts on philanthropic foundations, which typically provide clear guidelines on the type of proposals they will consider. With proposals to individuals, you can be more creative and less formal, but you also need to do a considerable amount of research to make sure you are crafting a proposal that will appeal to that particular donor's interests.

Individual donors are worth the effort. They consistently provide approximately three-quarters of all charitable giving in the United States, according to the annual Giving USA report, researched by the Indiana University Center on Philanthropy and published by the Giving USA Foundation. ■

the three 'c's' of prospect research

Prospect research refers to the process of evaluating prospective major-gift donors to determine how likely they are to support your institution and what level of giving is realistic. Information gleaned through this process is essential to developing targeted fundraising proposals and one-on-one solicitations that will help motivate prospects to contribute to your cause.

Keep these three factors in mind when conducting prospect research:

1. What is the prospect's connection to your institution? What would motivate the prospect to give? Is he a grateful patient of your health center? Is she an alumna of your university? Has the couple volunteered for your organization for many years?
2. What is the prospect's capacity to give? Research tools are available to help you determine your prospect's wealth, stock and real estate holdings, etc., so that the amount of support you ask for is in the right ballpark. Ask for too much and you may turn off your potential donor. Ask for too little and you've lost an opportunity for major support.
3. What does the prospect care about? Is he passionate about protecting the environment? Is name recognition an important concern? Is she an animal-rights activist?

For an extensive list of prospect research resources, visit www.aprahome.org/researchlinks/.

stewardship strategies

The most reliable source for future gifts to your organization is from the donors who already support you. It's vitally important that they understand how much you value their contributions, and the best way to let them know you appreciate their support is to communicate with them on a regular basis. Many large nonprofits have staff dedicated specifically to this task. But no matter how small your institution, donor stewardship should be a top priority.

Stewardship programs have three basic components:

- Acknowledgment – thanking donors early, often and appropriately for their level of support
- Recognition – publicly acknowledging a donor's generosity through a newsletter profile, honor roll, naming opportunity or invitation to a special event
- Reporting – reminding donors of the impact of their giving to set the stage for future support and provide accountability

producing effective proposals

Whether you're writing to an individual donor, a foundation or a corporation, keep the following tips in mind as you prepare your proposal:

- Plan as far in advance as possible so that appropriate time is available for research, writing, editing, approvals, revisions and packaging.
- Look at priority projects that have yet to be funded and begin the process of developing boilerplate proposals. If you've already agreed internally on the basics, you'll be able to move more quickly as prospects are identified. The boilerplate can then be tailored for individual prospects.
- The prospect will determine the tone and focus of the proposal. Two proposals to fund the same project often have a different emphasis. For example, a proposal to a medical school alumnus interested in perpetuating the name of a mentor will be very different from a proposal to a foundation, even if both proposals are targeted for cancer research.
- Foundations generally provide clear guidelines for what proposals they will accept and the format, structure and contents they require. Follow their guidelines closely.
- Every proposal should be highly readable, well-organized, persuasive, substantive and error-free.
- A proposal should be both concise and complete. Don't inundate the reader with excessive or repetitive information. On the other hand, don't provide too little explanation to a donor simply because you think that individual already knows the rationale for the project.
- Answer the basic questions: who, what, when, where, why and how. Lead the prospect in a logical order through the rationale for support.
- Let the donor know what difference the gift would make, both to the organization and, more importantly, to the donor.
- Avoid superlatives and meaningless generalities such as "the organization is a leader," unless you can back up the statement with concrete data. Most prospects are too savvy to fall for pure hyperbole.
- Avoid jargon. Be straightforward in presenting the information.
- Remember that money goes to strength. Instead of writing about needs and problems, discuss opportunities and potential.

seven thank yous

When it comes to donor relations, the fundamental rule is that you can't say thank you often enough.

Following are seven golden opportunities for thanking donors:

- a thank-you note with an enclosed photo following an event
- a thank-you letter following a one-on-one meeting, visit or lunch
- a thank-you call from your chief executive or the chair of your board after the donor pledges a gift
- a thank-you letter officially acknowledging that pledge, each future pledge payment and completion of the pledge
- listing the donor's gift in your honor roll (after obtaining permission through a letter that, again, thanks the donor for the gift)
- periodic reports on how the gift is being used
- a profile of the donor in your newsletter or on your Web site (again, with the donor's approval)

roadside assistance

Writing for a Good Cause: The Complete Guide to Crafting Proposals and Other Persuasive Pieces for Nonprofits
by Joseph and Danielle S. Barbato (2000)

Winning Grants Step-by-Step: The Complete Workbook for Planning, Developing and Writing Successful Proposals
by Mim Carlson (2002)

The Foundation Center's Guide to Proposal Writing
by Jane C. Cheever (2001)

The Artful Journey: Cultivating and Soliciting the Major Gift
by William T. Sturtevant (1997)

electronic media

survey says: LESS THAN 40% OF YOU CURRENTLY PRODUCE E-NEWSLETTERS, YET ALL SEE ITS GROWING IMPORTANCE.

THE INTERNET is changing so rapidly that new tools for electronic communication are coming online every day. You have to be nimble to stay ahead of the curve – or at least not too far behind it. The first and sometimes hardest step is collecting e-mail addresses.

Be sure to include an e-mail request line on all forms and cards in which you ask for other address information, and an e-mail opt-in box on your Web site. Encourage your audiences to visit your Web site by publishing your URL on all printed communications and stationery.

Be thoughtful in how you gather information on your constituents. You need to assure your audiences that you will manage their personal information confidentially. Make it crystal clear that you will not share their information with other organizations and that you will guard their privacy. Be true to your word. And give them an opportunity to opt out of your communications — and keep to that promise as well.

Maintaining your e-mail address list with accurate information can be challenging, as e-mail addresses change even faster than mailing addresses. Be sure your service provider has tools that automatically remove invalid addresses from your list. Every e-mail you send should have a link that makes it easy for your audiences to update their information.

Once you have your database of e-mail addresses, you'll want to look at options for communicating with your audiences electronically. Following are some of the most frequently used tools:

E-newsletters or e-zines are regularly distributed headlines and blurbs that often link to a Web site with more complete stories. Keep subject lines short, hyperlinks plentiful and graphics on your e-newsletter simple; otherwise, many in your audience won't have the patience to wait for your newsletter to load, or you'll clog their in-boxes. Either scenario may lead your readers to opt out of your mailing list.

Be sure you have enough staff, and enough news, to produce your e-newsletter in a timely fashion. And remember that although electronic newsletters save money on printing and postage costs, they often take as much time and effort to produce as print newsletters.

E-mail campaigns involve sending a series of targeted messages to a segment of your audience. For instance, you might undertake a campaign to help pass a particular piece of legislation; raise money for a special program or project; increase the membership level of a certain set of donors; or solicit volunteers for an upcoming event.

Viral marketing refers to the process of getting individuals to pass on your marketing message electronically to their friends, family and colleagues. It originated with the Hotmail marketing campaign that offered free e-mail in exchange for the automatic inclusion of a brief tagline/pitch at the bottom of each e-mail message sent via a Hotmail account. The Hotmail campaign was wildly successful, with some 12 million new subscribers in a year and a half. ■

> "Truly interactive e-mail campaigns can create a strong emotional bond with an organization," says Wharton marketing professor David Schmittlein. "That kind of use of e-mail is going to be growing, and it's going to have real economic return for organizations." For example, an orchestra could use its mailing list to tell subscribers about concerts, offer exclusive opportunities to meet performers and solicit opinions that would actually affect the next season's schedule.

getting your message through

E-mail users and networks are fighting back hard against spam. So how can you make sure your message gets through? Here are a few tips:

- Make sure you're only sending e-mail (including e-newsletters, e-zines and the like) to those who have requested it. Obtain permission before you send e-mails to even longtime supporters. And always include an easy unsubscribe option.
- Both your display name and e-mail address should accurately identify your organization. Most spam comes from individuals.
- Send your e-newsletters on a regular schedule so they are expected. They'll be more likely to be read that way.
- Be aware of the latest spam themes (mortgage rates, prescriptions, etc.) and avoid using them or related words in your copy.
- Test whether your message will get bounced. Establish e-mail accounts at some prominent e-mail and Internet Service Providers and send yourself the message to see if it goes through.
- A popular trend in spam monitoring is the "challenge-response system," which requires an e-mail sender to complete a specific task before any other e-mails are accepted from that sender. The task usually requires a human response – such as clicking on a link. This strategy reduces spamming, since spammers rely on automation for distribution of their messages.

roadside assistance

www.onphilanthropy.com
www.online-publishers.org
www.marketingprofs.com
www.newstips.org

Unleashing the Idea Virus
by Seth Godin and
Malcolm Gladwell (2001)

*101 Ways to Boost Your
Web Traffic: Internet Marketing
Made Easier, 3rd Edition*
by Thomas Wong (2004)

events

survey says: 61% OF YOU RATE SPECIAL EVENTS AS VITAL OR VERY USEFUL.

THE FIRST STEP in planning any event is knowing what you want to accomplish. Events can help you increase your visibility, attract prospective donors, improve community relations and/or thank existing donors. But events can be expensive, so know the potential cost and your alternatives for achieving the same goals before you commit to an event.

Whether your event is a black-tie dinner, conference for 1,000 or an intimate reception or lecture, choose your speakers strategically and plan well in advance for maximum publicity opportunities, before, during and after your event. (See the Media Relations section of this chapter for tips on enhancing your media coverage.) Use the opportunity of a captive audience to obtain contact information, including e-mail addresses, from attendees. And to greatly increase the impact of your event, follow up with attendees afterward.

> Events can be expensive, so know the cost and expected return before you commit to an event.

Events are labor-intensive activities, and paying attention to the small details is crucial. For example, despite an otherwise stellar event, your guests' prominent memory may be that the coffee was cold, the music was too loud or the speaker was inaudible because the microphone didn't work. Make your expectations clear to your caterer and other vendors before the event. Stage a rehearsal to test the sound and other AV equipment. (The pocket of this book contains an event checklist to help you keep track of the details.)

Be sure to send invitations out six to eight weeks in advance so that your invitees won't think they were last-minute additions to the guest list. And "save-the-date" cards or letters sent out 12 or more weeks in advance can help boost attendance. ■

leverage the impact of your events

- Brief your CEO and key volunteers on what you hope to accomplish by their interaction with VIP guests. Provide background information on important attendees.
- Use your key organizational messages to create talking points for informal conversations with VIPs and for media interviews.
- Arrange your seating plan strategically. Who should sit with which donors? With media? With other VIPs?
- If the event is newsworthy, pitch the story to your key media contacts and send out a media advisory. Have press kits ready and be sure to have the appropriate feeds if you anticipate broadcast coverage.
- Provide "for more information" cards to help build your database. Be sure to ask for e-mail addresses as well.
- Conduct a dress rehearsal before and a debriefing afterward, to get everything right this time and to do an even better job next time.
- Follow up after the event by sending guests photos, speech reprints, press clippings, etc., along with a note of thanks for attending. Don't forget to follow up with those who could not attend.

star-struck or star-stuck?

When you need to pull cameras into a room, few things are as magnetic as stars. Celebrities can spotlight your cause or make you pull your hair out. Author Andy Goodman reviews the rules of "celebrity engagement":

1. Find the right celebrity for the right cause – make sure the star is a good fit for your cause.
2. Find the right person to talk to – agent, manager, publicist, attorney, spouse.
3. Make your request clear, concise and in writing.
4. Have celebrities speak as informed citizens, not experts.
5. No surprises. Nothing fouls a relationship faster than a deviation from the agreed plan.
6. Thank you, thank you, thank you. After the celebrity's time has been donated, thank-you notes (or gifts) are in order for both the star and the handler.
7. Be careful. Celebrity spokespersons bring their own set of risks. They can eat up time and require careful attention.

Source: Andy Goodman, agoodmanonline.com

top speechwriting tips

- Find out as much as possible about your audience. Are they new to your organization or are they longtime supporters?
- Know your objective. Do you want to educate, motivate, inspire? What is the key message you want to impart?
- Make sure your goals and audience expectations mesh.
- Does your speaker prefer a fully written speech or bullet points to use as a guide?
- Keep your remarks short and focused, and use repetition to make your main message crystal clear.
- Tell a story. Paint a picture. Make it memorable.
- An effective presentation needs a beginning, middle and end, taking the listener on a logical progression as you develop and convey your message.
- Watch your language. Use transitional phrases to move forward. Use the active rather than the passive voice. And avoid overuse of "I" and unnecessary adverbs such as "very."
- Include a pronunciation guide for difficult names.

see event-planning checklist in the back pocket

roadside assistance

Special Events: Proven Strategies for Nonprofit Fundraising
by Alan L. Wendroff (2003)

Lend Me Your Ears
by William Safire (1997)

GALA: The Special Events Planner for Professionals & Volunteers
by Patti Coons and Lois M. Baron (1999)

Event planning books
by Judy Allen

www.abacon.com/pubspeak
www.public-speaking.org

guerilla marketing

survey says: MOST OF YOU HAVE NEVER CONDUCTED "GUERILLA MARKETING" CAMPAIGNS.

"GUERILLA MARKETING" uses fast, unconventional methods, often combined with a sense of humor, to accomplish conventional goals. It's all about thinking up creative ways to get your message out to your audience and to move them to action quickly, whether it's making a gift, signing a petition or attending an event. Guerilla marketing offers an irresistible combination of being inexpensive and innovative, which can lead to enhanced media visibility and word-of-mouth advertising.

> Tens of thousands of commuters saw the 'Hearses on the Highway.' Within a 24-hour period, calls to the EPA spiked 47 percent.

Andy Goodman used a guerilla tactic – a mock funeral procession of five hearses on a freeway during rush hour – to help an alliance of environmental organizations communicate with concerned citizens in Southern California. Each hearse had a billboard with a message about the health problems associated with air pollution in the region, and the last hearse included a toll-free hotline number at the Environmental Protection Agency.

"Tens of thousands of commuters saw the 'Hearses on the Highway' firsthand as they crept along with drive-time traffic, and millions more heard the story on morning radio or saw it on the local evening news programs," recalls Goodman. "Within a 24-hour period, calls to the EPA hotline from irate Angelenos demanding cleaner air spiked 47 percent. The total cost of the tactic: less than $2,000."

After years of litigation against Yum Brands (parent company of KFC Corporation) for inhumane practices, People for the Ethical Treatment of Animals received major media coverage and swift corporate response when it released footage of these practices from a hidden camera placed by one of its members in a West Virginia chicken slaughterhouse. Yum Brands threatened to cancel its contract with the plant, owned by Pilgrim's Pride, if conditions were not drastically improved. According to *The New York Times*, which extensively covered the story, "Pilgrim's Pride fired 11 workers and managers and said it would make everyone at its 25 plants sign promises to treat animals humanely." PETA then partnered with the Humane Society of America to ask Congress to amend the Humane Methods of Slaughter Act to include poultry.

In a less dramatic but similarly effective effort, Planned Parenthood of New England used coasters in bars and personal ads in newspapers to convey a series of hip and audience-appropriate pitches to address health concerns. The organization also was able to save significant money by using audience research that had already been conducted for a campaign to a demographically similar audience in Louisiana.

The best guerilla tactics not only reach your target audience, but also create buzz about your marketing campaign, your cause and your organization. The more inspired your approach, the more likely you are to draw media coverage and public interest. ■

> Among the many and varied channels through which a person today may receive information, it is hard to imagine any that carry the credibility and, as a result, the importance of interpersonal communication, or word-of-mouth. There is little debate as to whether word-of-mouth matters. In fact, there is good reason to believe it has more potential impact than any other communication channel.
>
> *Source: Harvard Business School Working Paper "Using Online Communication to Study Word of Mouth Communication," by David Godes of Harvard Business School and Dina Mayzlin of Yale's School of Management (2003)*

some guerilla tactics

- Print your key messages on buttons, T-shirts, bar coasters, banners, employee uniforms, decks of cards, flyers, posters, you name it.
- Turn your vehicles into movable billboards with car magnets, bumper stickers or hand-painted messages.
- Paint a mural on the side of your building or create window displays highlighting your organization. Or see if you may paint or post your message in the windows of community businesses.
- Hold a contest to draw new constituents to your organization.
- Shout your message through a bullhorn on the street corner or from a moving vehicle.
- Increase visibility for your nonprofit by speaking at community meetings, at other gatherings such as conferences, or door-to-door throughout the community.
- Display your materials at trade shows, via doorhangers (left at people's homes in your target area) and in all of your facilities (through "take-one" boxes or periodical displays).
- Produce an infomercial.
- Include key messages on your voice-mail system and on-hold programming on your phones.
- Spread positive word-of-mouth through your volunteers, employees, donors and student interns.

roadside assistance

Guerilla Marketing
www.gmarketing.com
(*Web site of guerilla marketing pioneer Jay Conrad Levinson*)

The Secrets of Master Marketing: Discover How To Produce an Endless Stream of New, Repeat and Referral Business by Using These Powerful Marketing and Customer Service Secrets
by *David L. Hancock (2003)*

The World's Best Known Marketing Secret: Building Your Business With Word-Of-Mouth Marketing
by *Ivan R. Misner and Virginia Devine (1999)*

marketing materials

survey says: 100% OF YOU PRODUCE SOME FORM OF MARKETING MATERIALS.

YOU CAN COMMUNICATE as much about your organization through the look and feel of your marketing materials as you can through the words they convey. To be noticed, read and remembered, your publications need to be visually appealing. To reinforce your brand identity, your materials need to be linked visually and express consistent messages. And, as in all other forms of communication, it is essential that you know your audience and what you hope to accomplish through each piece.

If you're hiring an outside designer, writer or photographer, make sure your vendor is a good fit (an event photographer may not be the best choice to shoot environmental portraits of donors, for instance). If you have the right people on board – and you've effectively communicated your goals, expectations and the parameters of the project – you should trust their counsel. Carefully negotiate usage rights to photography and design concepts at the outset, and include ancillary rights such as posting photographs on your Web site. Know exactly what rights you're paying for so you won't be surprised later. For printing, always obtain at least three bids and be sure you're comparing apples to apples.

> I've learned that you can't have **EVERYTHING** and do everything at the same time.
> oprah winfrey

In choosing the right mix of print materials for your needs, consider the frequency with which your organization has news to report. A newsletter or magazine requires a consistent flow of stories, while a brochure may be more effective in announcing a single new program. Since funding sources often require audited financial statements, many nonprofits turn their annual report into an opportunity to highlight the organization's accomplishments and vision for the future. This strategy can give you extra bang for your buck, since you can make dual use of the publication as a tool for attracting new prospects. And once you launch a successful periodical, produce it on a consistent schedule to maintain interest. ■

low-budget, high-impact ideas

- Hire a designer to create a template that you can fill in for subsequent issues. This gives you a professional design at a reduced cost, but be sure you have the skill and training to pull off completion of the project in-house.
- Submit final copy to your designer, not copy that's still a work in progress. Otherwise, you'll be paying for lots of unnecessary corrections.
- If you can't afford new photography from cover to cover, invest in a few professional shots and run them larger.
- Choosing the right paper will save you big bucks (paper is 25 percent of the cost of most print pieces). Look at the "house stock" paper your printer uses. You can sometimes achieve a similar look at a significantly lower cost.
- Use standard-size paper and eliminate high-end bells and whistles (die-cuts, full-page bleeds, embossing).
- Most printing presses are configured to handle an even number of colors (two, four or six colors), so it's more cost-effective to specify colors in pairs. Varnish counts as a color.
- Determine your print quantity carefully. The cost of producing 10,000 copies all at once is significantly less than printing 5,000 copies two separate times, but you don't want to be stuck with publications you won't use.
- If you need to produce dual-language marketing publications, instead of printing two different pieces, it can be cost-effective to print the English version and the other language side by side (or one on the front, the other on the back), using the same photographs.
- Use color printers and copiers to give even your lowest-budget pieces a more polished look.

push vs. pull

Many nonprofits, as well as corporations, use a combination of Web and print as a powerful "push/pull" mix to communicate with current stakeholders while drawing new ones. Your direct-mail pieces, whether a print newsletter, magazine, a fundraising appeal or an e-mail announcement, "push" your message to current audiences, while Web sites and brochures help "pull" in new audiences.

print and web publishing pluses and minuses

print:

+	−
Control over look and feel	Expensive
Control over distribution	Time-consuming
Tangible	Less flexible
More personal	Difficult, expensive to change
Compact and portable	Price fluctuations
Preferred by readers	

web:

+	−
Can be created and posted quickly	Lack of control over look and feel
Can be changed and updated easily	Audience must be made aware it exists
Interactive	Intangible/ephemeral
Unlimited space	Impersonal
Flexibility in number of pages presented	
Relatively inexpensive	

roadside assistance

Getting It Printed: How to Work With Printers and Graphic Imaging Services to Assure Quality, Stay on Schedule and Control Costs
by Mark Beach and Eric Kenly (1999)

Graphic Designer's Digital Printing and Prepress Handbook
by Constance Sidles (2001)

Publishing the Nonprofit Annual Report: Tips, Traps, and Tricks of the Trade
by Caroline Taylor (2001)

Alleviating Prepress Anxiety: How to Manage Your Print Projects for Savings, Schedule and Quality
by Ann Goodheart (2000)

The Society of Publication Designers 39th Publication Design Annual
by George Lois (2004)

See the section on Web sites for Web publishing resources.

media relations

survey says: 86% OF YOU SEE MEDIA RELATIONS AS AN IMPORTANT TOOL.

ONE OF THE FASTEST ways to build awareness of your organization among mass audiences is by obtaining press coverage. "Earned" media, placing news and feature stories in print, broadcast and electronic media, is more credible and less expensive than paying for advertising, but you have limited control over how your message will be delivered.

As you begin planning your media relations effort, know what you want to accomplish and who you want to reach. Do you want to increase the general visibility and reputation of your organization? Do you want to attract new donors and volunteers to your food bank? Do you want to increase your university's ranking in *U.S. News and World Report*? Your goals should be realistic and clearly defined. You also should develop two or three messages that succinctly convey your position and/or your organization's strengths and accomplishments.

> **"PUBLIC RELATIONS"** includes media, community, government and donor relations. **"MEDIA RELATIONS"** specifically refers to working with print, broadcast and electronic media.

Next, you need to ask yourself: "Who can help my organization achieve its goals?" and "What kinds of media do they listen to, watch or read?"

Most media outlets maintain extensive demographic information that they use to boost their advertising sales. This information is readily available – often on the Web – and also can be used to prioritize among the news media that reach your key audiences for purposes of news and feature pitches. While national media and your local daily newspaper reach wider audiences, it's often more effective for nonprofits to target community-based and ethnic media. Sometimes these smaller news outlets allow you to reach your key audiences with greater precision and efficacy.

ethnic and gay/lesbian media

Including ethnic and gay/lesbian media in your communications plans can be a vital tool for reaching key constituent groups. A report by New California Media, based on a survey of 2,000 ethnic households in 12 languages, found "some 84 percent of Hispanic, Asian and African-American residents of California (close to 17 million) access ethnic media outlets regularly, and 54 percent cite a specific TV or radio program, Web site or publication as their primary source for news every day."

The U.S. Census Bureau's June 2004 ethnicity statistics confirmed the increasing diversity of the U.S. population, with the number of Latinos and Asians growing approximately four times faster than the overall population during the past three years. And, according to 2000 U.S. Census data, gays and lesbians make up at least 10 percent or more of the American population.

A comprehensive listing of more than 1,800 ethnic print, broadcast and electronic media organizations in the United States is available through the NCM Directory at www.NCMonline.com/directory.

Other relevant resources include:

- Asian American Journalists Association, www.aaja.org
- Native American Journalists Association, www.naja.com
- National Association of Black Journalists, www.nabj.org
- National Gay and Lesbian Task Force, www.ngltf.org
- National Association of Hispanic Journalists, www.nahj.org
- National Association of Minority Media Executives, www.namme.org/

tracking your coverage

Keep a record of your success. You may need assistance in the collection of media coverage, especially for Internet articles and broadcast pieces, as they can disappear quickly. Volunteers and interns can help, or you can use a clipping service. For a list of services that track print, broadcast and Internet coverage, try www.clippingservice.com. Other sources include:

- www.bacons.com
- www.burrellesluce.com
- www.lexisnexis.com/currentawareness/trackers
- www.webclipping.com

components of a media relations plan

- Goals
- Target audiences
- Key messages
- News hooks/pitch angles and corresponding timeline
- Media contact/distribution list
- Deliverables (press kit, releases, op-ed articles, etc.)
- Media training
- Tracking coverage

who do you call?

Start building relationships with media by becoming a media consumer — watch TV news, listen to the news radio stations, and browse news Web sites and relevant newspapers and magazines. Take note of the media outlets/reporters who cover the issues related to your cause. Most media outlets have a reporter/section dedicated to nonprofit/charitable activities. Try the News section on Google to locate recent news stories on issues relevant to your organization. If your budget permits, you can also invest in a subscription to news archive databases such as Factiva or Lexis-Nexis.

roadside assistance

SPIN Works!
by Robert Bray (2002)
www.spinproject.org
http://aboutpublicrelations.net
www.aboutpr.com
www.prsa.org
www.prweb.com

Media Relations Handbook for Agencies, Associations, Nonprofits and Congress
by Brad Fitch (2004)

The Fall of Advertising and the Rise of PR
by Al and Laura Ries (2002)

media: pitching your story

survey says: 60% OF YOU WOULD LIKE TO IMPROVE YOUR ABILITY TO SECURE PRESS COVERAGE.

TO IMPLEMENT your media plan effectively, you must actively cultivate relationships with reporters and editors. Editors need good stories as much as nonprofits need media coverage, but the way in which nonprofits define a "good story" often differs from that of news outlets.

To position your institution as a valued news source, it's essential to pitch only stories that are truly newsworthy and a good fit with the media outlet. For instance, you wouldn't pitch a story on the shortage of affordable housing to a health care reporter (unless, of course, you found a great angle, such as unsanitary or dangerous living conditions in inner-city housing). Be objective: If you were not involved in your cause, would you find the story interesting?

Don't succumb to internal pressure to pitch stories that are not newsworthy. Not only will the story be turned down, but you also run the risk of damaging your relationship with the news outlet. While a million-dollar gift may be a big deal to your organization, it's not inherently newsworthy.

> Who can help my organization **ACHIEVE** its goals?
>
> What kinds of media do they listen to, watch or read?

Familiarize yourself thoroughly with the media in which you want to appear and think creatively about potential news angles and hooks: What makes your story worth telling *now*? Are you releasing a new report? Informing the public about a new program or service? Publicizing the local impact of a national court decision, new law or national news event? Also consider pitching to entertainment programs. Boston Latin School, in the midst of its first fundraising campaign, earned a favorable mention on *The West Wing* in an episode centering on public education. And don't forget to include op-ed articles in your media efforts.

You probably already have an "in" with the media that you're not aware of. Have you asked your volunteers or board members if they have friends in the media? Chances are that they do. Ask around and then leverage these relationships as much as possible. ∎

e-mail, fax or snail-mail?

- Use e-mail for print publications and Web sites. Summarize pitch in subject heading. Make sure your e-mail doesn't look like spam.
- Use fax for TV newsrooms, which are too busy to sort through e-mail.
- Reserve snail-mail for press kit mailings, if you're trying to build a long-term relationship with an editor or in preparation of a feature pitch. Call the editor beforehand to make sure it's OK to send. Unwarranted mail solicitations will most likely go in the trash.
- Follow up your pitch with a phone call, but be sure you're not calling close to deadline.

> Have a media-friendly Web site with current biographical information, organizational history, downloadable photographs, news archives, press clippings and other relevant information to increase your value as a news source. An online experts directory, ideally with video clips of your top spokespeople, can help you generate even more media coverage.

building a media list

Pay services are available to supplement your efforts or to help you develop an entire database from scratch. It pays to comparison-shop and to verify the information with the individual media outlets. Some services are updated more frequently than others and offer a variety of delivery mechanisms (printed book, CD-ROM, Web site). These services typically maintain circulation and demographic information on media outlets as well.

Following are a few well-known suppliers of media contact information:

- Bacon's Media Directories, www.bacons.com
- Burrelle's Media Directory, www.burrelles.com
- Gebbie Press, www.gebbieinc.com
- News Media Yellow Book, Leadership Directories, www.leadershipdirectories.com
- The Capital Source, National Journal, Washington, D.C.

> Video/audio news releases (VNRs) – shot in the format of a news story – can be effective tools for educating people and building awareness. They are expensive, so do a cost/benefit analysis and make sure your story is truly newsworthy before making an investment.

media alerts

A media advisory calls attention to upcoming events, news conferences or briefings. It describes the event in much less detail than a press release. Media advisories should be sent to your key media contacts and also placed in "daybooks" and in "week-ahead columns." Daybooks are daily calendars of events compiled by newswire services and published for national, state and major-city markets. Week-ahead columns serve the same purpose in smaller markets. Send media advisories out the week before your event and again one or two days before as a reminder.

A media advisory should be clearly identified as such. It should include no more than one or two paragraphs describing the event – with an emphasis on why it merits coverage – and the specifics: date, time, location, contact information, your organization and any key participants (who, what, when, where, why and how). Don't forget to include a headline as well.

see news release guidelines in the back pocket

roadside assistance
www.ap.org
www.reuters.com
www.prnewswire.com
www.businesswire.com

web sites: creating and maintaining

survey says: 85% OF YOU SAY A WEB SITE IS VITAL TO YOUR ORGANIZATION, YET LESS THAN 10% TEST THE SITE WITH VISITORS PRIOR TO LAUNCH.

WITH SOME 400 million people (and counting) online worldwide today, the first place many of us look for information is the Internet. As you design a Web site for your organization, keep a few fundamental rules in mind. Remember, on the Web, people don't read; they scan. Good sites are easy to navigate, are clearly and consistently organized, and have robust search functions.

If it's a choice between simple and easy-to-use vs. complex with lots of bells and whistles, opt for simplicity every time. Sites that take too long to load can turn off many users. You may attract people to your site once, but they won't come back if it's too difficult to use.

Maintaining your Web site is at least as important as creating it in the first place. Add new content regularly, or at least indicate that the site has been reviewed and updated recently. Write Web-friendly (i.e., concise, clear) text and proofread your site as carefully as you would a print publication. Even though it's easy to make corrections, a site with errors can make users lose confidence in the quality of your organization. And avoid the common mistake of simply posting Web versions of your brochures online.

Fortunately, you no longer have to know HTML (hypertext markup language) to update a Web site. Instead, you'll want to use a content management system (CMS) to help you keep your site current. CMS makes it simpler for those unfamiliar with HTML to post and update materials without assistance from technical staff. And because CMS relies on templates, it helps ensure a consistent look and feel to your Web pages.

Finally – and we can't stress this enough – you must design your Web site so that it is search-engine friendly. You may have an incredible site, but if it pops up as item number 1,723 or 1,723,000 in a Google search, it will be tough for people to find. For more on search-engine optimization, the term for increasing your visibility on Web search engines, read on. ■

testing your site

According to Web usability expert Steve Krug: "If you want a great site, you've got to test. Testing one user is 100 percent better than testing none. Testing one user early in the project is better than testing 50 near the end."

Although Krug believes focus groups are great for testing the names of features on your site and for providing general information about audience preferences, he says they shouldn't be mistaken for usability testing. "The kinds of things you can learn from focus groups are the things you need to learn early on, before you begin designing the site," he says. "But they're not good for learning about whether your site works and how to improve it. They won't tell you whether people can actually use your site."

To effectively test usability, you need to recruit a few representatives of your target audience and observe them, one at a time, as they try to complete a specific task on your Web site. For example, you may ask participants how they would go about making an online gift, or finding news about upcoming events, and observe how easy or difficult it is for them to navigate through the process. This kind of testing is both inexpensive and invaluable in ensuring that your site is easy for your key audiences to use.

> According to a Nielsen//Net Ratings report in March 2004, some 204.3 million Americans, 75 percent of the citizenry, have home Internet access, an increase of 9 percent over the prior year. "In just a handful of years, online access has managed to gain the type of traction that took other media decades to achieve," said Kenneth Cassar, Nielsen's director of strategic analysis.
>
> Nielsen also reports that Web surfers are more politically active than the general population.

great web sites

Looking for inspiration as you create or update your Web site? Check out these nominees for the International Academy of Digital Arts & Sciences' 2004 Webby Awards, dubbed by *The New York Times* as "The Oscars of the Internet."

- www.aworldconnected.com
- http://blogforamerica.com
- www.cancerfacts.com
- www.earthisland.org
- www.exploratorium.edu
- www.gracecathedral.org
- www.hivstopswithme.org
- www.hrc.org
- www.indybay.org
- www.kidshealth.org
- www.myjewishlearning.com
- www.tolerance.org

to blog or not to blog

Blogs are one of the hottest trends on the Web today. Short for weblogs, blogs are proliferating because they're among the least expensive, easiest and fastest ways to share information. Blogs send your content directly to your audience whenever new information is posted on your site. They also allow for instant feedback, making them invaluable in building relationships with your key audiences. And because content is frequently updated, blogs can increase your ranking in Internet search engines.

To build awareness of your blog's existence, post its headlines on your organization's Web site, send out an e-mail and/or announcement of your blog, and ask partner organizations to link to your site.

Free automated publishing systems, such as www.blogger.com, can help you set up a blog in just a few minutes. Free news readers also are readily available, although you need to choose the right one for your computer operating system. For the Mac, try http://ranchero.com/netnewswire/; for Microsoft Outlook, www.newsgator.com is a good option; www.feedreader.com is a freeware application for Windows; and www.bloglines.com is a Web-based reader.

But before you launch a blog, be sure you will have enough regular new content to make it worthwhile. To be effective, a blog must be updated regularly – at least two or three times per week, if not daily.

Be aware that whoever writes your blog will effectively be speaking for the entire organization. Proceed with caution. Just because blogging is a new trend doesn't mean it's right for your organization.

roadside assistance

Don't Make Me Think!: A Common Sense Approach to Web Usability
by Steve Krug (2000)

Homepage Usability: 50 Homepages Deconstructed
by Jakob Nielsen and Marie Tahir (2001)

Information Architecture for the World Wide Web
by Louis Rosenfeld and Peter Morville (2002)

Information Architecture: Blueprints for the Web
by Christina Wodtke (2002)

web sites: optimization

survey says: MOST OF YOU SEE ONLINE GIVING AS A GROWING NECESSITY.

NO MATTER how good your content and your Web site, if it is buried among hundreds – or thousands – of other sites, it's not going to be very effective. Studies show that more than 85 percent of Web surfers use search engines every day. If the most widely used search engines don't list your organization's site on the first couple of pages of their results, chances are your message is not going to get through.

In addition to creating your Web site so that it ranks high in search engines (see sidebar), it's crucial that you keep foremost in mind the needs and preferences of your target audience. Give users confidence in the quality of your site by keeping the information accurate and up-to-date, by frequently checking to make sure you have no broken links, and by giving them an easy way to make a gift or connect with a real person if they need additional information or assistance.

Continue your usability testing when you make any significant changes to your site. And use tracking software to help measure your results. Remember that tracking usage of your Web site is as critical to building an effective communications program as tracking your direct-mail results. ∎

seven key factors in search engine optimization

Search engines rank your site on a number of factors, namely "keywords" – the words most frequently mentioned on your site. Following are the seven key factors to keep in mind to increase your search engine ranking:

1. Title tag – The title tag is like a master keyword; it's the first thing a search engine displays after you enter a search request. Every single Web page should have its own title tag, and it should be the exact keyword you used for the Web page you are trying to optimize. Avoid generic keywords; choose only those appropriate for your organization.
2. ALT tags – Also put your main keyword(s) in the ALT tags on your images.
3. Link popularity – Most search engines won't consider a Web site unless at least one or two links point to it. Your keywords should be in those links. Before linking with other sites, check them out to ensure they don't have hidden text or repeat keywords (considered spam by search engines).
4. Keyword density – Your keyword should appear once in the title tag, once in the heading tag, once in the bold text, and in the first and last sentence of the page. But don't overdo the frequency of your keywords. Overuse can be interpreted by search engines as spam.

5. Rich theme – Search engines are increasingly looking at themes in Web sites. Create as much content as possible (FAQs, articles, tips, etc.), and keep Web pages to between 200 and 500 words. The more pages you have that are related to your "theme" and that include your keywords, the more likely you'll be successful in your ranking.
6. In-site cross-linking – Link to topic-related content across your site to enhance your theme. Every page should link back to your home page, and none of the pages on your site should be more than three clicks away from the home page.
7. Web site design – Text should outweigh HTML content. Make sure your pages are viewable in all leading-edge browsers, and stay away from Flash and Java Script, which are not favored by search engines because they are slow to load on many computers.

Source: Jeff Solomon, ThinkLogic LLC

using listservs

A listserv is an electronic mailing list that allows specific audiences or online communities to exchange ideas and information quickly and easily. Questions and answers submitted by members of the list automatically are e-mailed to everyone on the listserv.

Nonprofits can use listservs in a variety of ways:

- As a forum for feedback from constituents on services provided by the nonprofit
- As an advocacy tool to build a grassroots effort to influence legislation or spread the word about a particular issue
- To communicate with partner organizations and peer institutions about common issues and concerns

Check out eModerators, a resource for people who facilitate online discussion groups, at www.emoderators.com/moderators.shtml.

online giving

Online gifts to nonprofits increased by 48 percent during 2003, according to the *Chronicle of Philanthropy*'s fifth annual survey on the topic. The 157 nonprofits that participated in the survey received more than $100 million through Internet donations in 2003.

As this trend continues, more nonprofits are stepping up to the plate with more sophisticated Web sites and secure servers that support online giving. But you don't have to make a major investment to launch an online giving program. Many small nonprofits are taking advantage of www.paypal.com, a free, easy-to-set-up service initially used for e-commerce that also allows nonprofit donations to be made securely via the Web.

To make donors aware that you accept online gifts, you can send postcard announcements, publicize the program in your newsletter or e-mail your constituents. A common obstacle is that most nonprofits don't have e-mail addresses for their donors and prospects.

"There are no shortcuts to raising money online or offline," says Ted Hart, president and CEO of ePhilanthropy Foundation. "But with technology, there are more efficiencies and the opportunity to reach out to more people. And that is what should be drawing nonprofits to use the Internet."

"And contrary to the impression many have that online giving is dominated by people in their 20s, most donors are aged 30 to 59," he adds.

roadside assistance

Search Engine Optimization
www.searchenginestrategies.biz/index.htm and
www.searchenginewatch.com

Hot Text: Web Writing That Works
by Jonathan and Lisa Price (2002)

www.useit.com
Jakob Nielsen's Web Site includes *How Users Read on the Web* and *Applying Writing Guidelines to Web Pages.*

The Big Red Fez: How To Make Any Web Site Better
by Seth Godin (2002)

www.nyu.edu/library/resources/webwriting/, Bobst Library: Writing for the Web

www.sempo.org
SEMPO is a nonprofit professional association working to increase awareness and promote the value of search-engine marketing worldwide.

TOP TIPS

- To reinforce your brand identity, link materials visually and express consistent messages.

- Attract and retain donors through targeted messages aimed at their individual motivations for giving.

- Spend as much time maintaining your Web site as you spent launching it.

- Increase your ranking in Internet search engines by using key words.

- Collect e-mail addresses of your constituents at every opportunity.

- Build credibility/awareness through press coverage.

- Make sure your story is newsworthy, interesting and appropriate.

- Use advocacy to get your cause on the public agenda and shift the way stories on your issue are reported.

chapter five
are we there yet?

You've come a long way on your communications journey. Now it's time to assess the progress you've made and to consider ways to adjust your strategies for even greater success.

In this final chapter, we'll discuss how to measure the effectiveness of your efforts and enhance your accountability to your constituents while maintaining a more efficient and effective communications program. And let's face it, sometimes you're going to make mistakes along the way. We learn more from what doesn't work than from what does. The point is to continue to refine your efforts so that you develop the right communications mix that moves the goals of your mission forward.

measurement

survey says: ONLY 28% OF YOU CONSIDER MEASURING THE SUCCESS OF COMMUNICATIONS EFFORTS AS VITAL, YET MEASUREMENT OF SUCCESS IS A KEY ELEMENT OF ALL FUNDING GUIDELINES.

WHILE quantifying the impact of communications efforts can be challenging, it has its rewards. You'll be able to ascertain what's working and what's not so that you can make adjustments to your plan. You'll be able to demonstrate to your board, in concrete terms, the value of funding a comprehensive communications program for your organization. And you'll know that your efforts are making a real difference in reaching your constituents and supporting your nonprofit's mission.

So where do you start? To know where you are now, you need to know where you began. Of the few nonprofits that evaluate their communications programs, most forget the crucial step of establishing a baseline. Before you launch a new marketing program, survey your key audiences about their perceptions of your organization. Then conduct a similar survey after you launch a new publication or advocacy campaign to measure the difference your communication made to audience perceptions.

You also need to know your goals. If you want to increase major gifts from $3.5 million per year to $5 million per year, it will be much easier to measure your success than if you have a general goal of "raising more money." Similarly, if you want to increase attendance at your events from 350 to 400 people, you can quantify the results of the specific communications tools you use to attract new attendees.

Be sure to segment and test your vehicles along the way. For instance, if you are planning a direct-mail fundraising appeal, you should try out a couple of different approaches on select portions of your audience to determine which is likely to yield a higher response rate.

Measuring your organization in comparison with your peer institutions is another indicator of your success. In a blind survey, find out what the media thinks of your organization and others in your sphere. Track how that changes over time as you implement new media relations strategies. External evaluation sources also can provide valuable feedback, such as *U.S. News and World Report's* rankings of universities and hospitals.

If you're creative in your approach, you can usually think of useful measures for each of your communications projects. ■

tools for measuring results

Following are a few ideas for evaluating specific types of communications efforts:

MEDIA RELATIONS

Easily measurable media goals include "placement of 12 stories in major national media" or "achieving a total of 400 hits in external media." But how do you measure how well your message is being heard? If you're trying to shift the way the media report on your issue (as discussed in Chapter Four, Advocacy), track how often the media covering your organization are picking up your specific talking points (i.e., the key messages you include in your press releases or pitches and those your spokespersons say on camera). Is your success rate better if you have one-on-one meetings with the reporter?

CRISIS COMMUNICATIONS

With crisis communications, you can measure your effectiveness at preventing negative media coverage and the amount of revenue your nonprofit would have lost, from donors and other constituents, had you been unable to prevent a negative news report. For example, if there's a protest in front of your building and your efforts are responsible for keeping it out of the news, you can quantify the cost savings to your nonprofit and help make the case to your board for funding your media relations program.

PUBLICATIONS

Readership surveys can tell you what your audience thinks of the quality and frequency of your periodical, how much of it they read, whether they pass it on to friends and family, whether it motivates them to take action or make a gift, and many other valuable pieces of information. If you include a business-reply envelope that is coded for the specific publication, you can compare the response you receive to each of your publications.

WEB SITES

Many organizations count hits on their Web sites, but what does that really tell you? A large number of hits may actually indicate that your audience is having trouble finding the information they want. Because the Web is an interactive medium, it can be a great tool for obtaining direct feedback from your audience regarding what works – and what doesn't – on your site. Other measures include looking at usage patterns, such as peak usage times and what information people are accessing most. Also, it's a good idea to track changes in outcomes – how many donors are making a gift online compared with last year? How many gave before, and after, you sent a postcard attracting people to the site?

roadside assistance

Institute for Public Relations, www.instituteforpr.com (and its Commission on Public Relations Measurement and Evaluation)

How to Measure Your Communication Programs by Angela Sinickas (1994)

Measuring Brand Communication ROI by Don E. Schultz and Jeffrey S. Walters (1997)

refining/adjusting

survey says: VERY FEW OF YOU FUND A FORMAL ASSESSMENT PROCESS FOR COMMUNICATIONS INITIATIVES, YET ALL SEE THE IMPORTANCE OF MEASUREMENT.

NO MATTER how thoroughly you plan your trip, sometimes you have to change course. You need to stay flexible. And as the results and responses come in, you might need to shift gears and turn left instead of right.

Perhaps an arts organization may launch a major marketing push to expand its audience and sell more tickets. Or you may have a special fundraising event with a set number of available seats. You want to attract new attendees, but you don't want people to get frustrated if demand suddenly exceeds capacity. It's a fine line between creating buzz for a sold-out event and engendering bad word-of-mouth for building expectations in your audience, only to dash them.

> In the business world, the rearview mirror is always **CLEARER** than the windshield.
> famed wall street prognosticator warren buffett

Earlier in this book, we talked about preparing for success. But if you're even more successful than you thought, how can you readjust your plans to meet capacity? In the above scenarios, you can partner with other institutions to help handle your overflow. Or you can pitch a donor on funding a short-term and/or long-term solution, such as helping you lease a temporary space, underwriting additional performances or building a new facility.

It's also important for nonprofits to be able to respond quickly when events in popular culture or politics take a turn that can be advantageous to your organization. You have to pay attention to what's going on in the world around you and think creatively about how you can participate in the discussion to benefit your organization and those you serve.

In this book, we have covered most of the major tools nonprofits use to communicate with their audiences. While there's a logical progression, you need to conduct research and have a communications plan in place before you launch into implementation, it pays to go back over your tracks periodically. For instance, you should revisit your research and update your plan on a regular basis. Life happens, things change. Your planning documents will need to be amended periodically.

If you're doing something that doesn't work, change it. If it works well, do more of it. ■

the power of communications

A woman is driving alongside a river, looks over and sees a baby drowning. She pulls over, jumps in the river, grabs the baby and brings it ashore. But no sooner has she climbed up the bank, she looks back and sees another baby drowning. She jumps back in, grabs the baby, brings it to shore, and, oh no, there's another one. She goes in after it. And then there's another and another and, pretty soon, she's really busy saving babies one at a time.

A second woman passes by, sees the drowning babies and jumps in. The first woman sees that the second woman isn't bringing the babies out of the water and yells, "What are you doing?" The second woman says, "I'm teaching the babies how to swim!"

Just then, a third woman comes by, sees what's going on, but turns around and starts running in the other direction. The other women yell, "Where are you going?" She says, "I'm going upstream to stop whoever is throwing these babies into this river!"

Remember that by using strategic communications, you can get way past saving one baby at a time. In fact, you have the power to bring people together to solve some of the society's most pressing problems, shifting perceptions and creating positive social change on a massive scale. Enjoy your journey.

> We're taking our own advice and will be surveying our readers on ways we can improve this toolkit. We welcome your feedback and suggestions for future updates. E-mail us at toolkit@causecommunications.org.

roadside assistance

www.nationalresultscouncil.org

Begging for Change: The Dollars and Sense of Making Nonprofits Responsive, Efficient, and Rewarding for All by Robert Egger (2004)

Why Nonprofits Fail: Overcoming Founder's Syndrome, Fundphobia and Other Obstacles to Success by Stephen R. Block (2003)

Breakthrough Thinking for Nonprofit Organizations: Creative Strategies for Extraordinary Results (Jossey Bass Nonprofit & Public Management Series) by Bernard Ross and Clare Segal (2002)

High Performance Nonprofit Organizations: Managing Upstream for Greater Impact by Christine W. Letts, William P. Ryan and Allen Grossman (1998)

TOP TIPS

- You can't effectively measure where you end without first establishing where you started.

- Segment and test along the way.

- Benchmark your organization in comparison with peer institutions.

- If you're doing something that doesn't work, change it. If it works well, do more of it.

looking ahead

WE BELIEVE strongly in the transformative power of nonprofits in our society. In no other sector is the power to do good greater. And we know that by improving your communications efforts, nonprofits will thrive, change will be made and the world will be a better place.

We have devoted our lives to the field of communications. Over the years, we've provided all of the types of services outlined in this book and then some. And we've frequently been asked to compile our experiences and insights into a resource for others who are dedicated to improving nonprofit communications.

You have many choices in the way you approach your work. We hope you find this book both informative and useful as you find your own best path. ■

index

A

Aaker, David A., 13
abacon.com/pubspeak, 45
aboutpr.com, 51
aboutpublicrelations.net, 51
Ad Age, 33
Adler, Stephen, 33
advertising
    general, 32-33, 50
    online advertising, 33
    print, F
    public service announcements, 33
    television, 11, 32-33
Advertising Council, 17, 33
advertopedia.com, 33
advocacy, 34-35, 43
allaboutbranding.com, 13
Allen, Judy, 45
Alleviating Prepress Anxiety: How to Manage Your Print Projects for Savings, Schedule and Quality, 49
Alliance for Justice, G, 35
The Alliance of Nonprofit Mailers, 39
Alka Seltzer, 14
American Association of Advertising Agencies, 33
American Cancer Society, 35
American Heart Association, 33
American Heritage Dictionary, v
America SCORES, 29
Andringa, Robert C., 25
Annenberg Public Policy Center, 35
ap.org, 53
Applying Writing Guidelines to Web Pages, 57
aprahome.org, 40
The Artful Journey: Cultivating and Soliciting the Major Gift, 41
The Art of Cause Marketing, 29
Asian American Journalists Association, 51
Associated Press Stylebook, 15
@issue, M

audience
    perceptions, vi-vii, 4, 5, 6, 7, 12, 13, 24, 60
    researching, 4, 5, 16, 21
    segmenting/targeting, 10, 11, E, 50
audit, *see* communications audit
Austin, James E., 29
aworldconnected.com, 55

B

Baccarat, 23
bacons.com, 51, 53
Bacon's Media Directories, 53
"Backyard Wildlife Sanctuary" initiative, 29
Bancel, Marilyn, 37
Bang! Getting Your Message Heard in a Noisy World, 13
Barbato, Joseph and Danielle S., 41
Baron, Lois M., 45
Beach, Mark, 49
Beckwith, Harry, 4, 5
Bedbury, Scott, 12
Begging for Change: The Dollars and Sense of Making Nonprofits Responsive, Efficient, and Rewarding for All, 63
Bender, Dennis, 13
The Big Red Fez: How To Make Any Web Site Better, 57
Block, Stephen R., 63
blogforamerica.com, 55
blogger.com, 55
bloglines.com, 55
blogs, 55
boardcafe.org, 25
Board Source, 7
Bobst Library: Writing for the Web, 57
Boston Latin School, 52
Brand Aid, 13
brandchannel.com, 13
The Brand Gap, 13
branding, vi, 12-13, 16, E, 38, 48
Brand Leadership, 13
Bray, Robert, 51
Bread for the World, 14

Breakthrough Thinking for Nonprofit Organizations: Creative Strategies for Extraordinary Results, 63
Brice, Fanny, 4
Brown, John Seeley, 17
"buckle up" campaign, 17
budget
    allocation of resources, 10, 13, 20-27, 49
    buy-in, 13, 20, 24-25, 26-27
    percentage of operational budget, 23, 24
    pro-bono assistance, 22
    stretching limited dollars, 3, 20-25, 49
The Budget-Building Book for Nonprofits, 21
Budgeting for Not-For-Profit Organizations, 21
Buffett, Warren, 62
buildingbrands.com, D
Building Your Direct Mail Program, 39
Built to Last: Successful Habits of Visionary Companies, 7
burrellesluce.com, 51
Burrelle's Media Directory, 53
Bush, George W., 11
businesswire.com, 53

C

Campbell, Bruce, 5
cancerfacts.com, 55
capital campaigns, 24, 36-37
The Capital Source, 53
Carlson, Mim, 41
case statements, 36, 37
Casey, Mary Anne, 5
Cassar, Kenneth, 55
Cause Communications, F
Cause Marketing Forum, 29
cause-related marketing, 23, 28-29
celebrities, 45
Center for Media and Public Affairs, 34
Center on Philanthropy at Indiana University, 37, 40
Center for Science in the Public Interest, 17
Center for What Works, 7
Chappell, Tom, 6

Charity Navigator, 7
Cheever, Jane, 41
Chicago Manual of Style, 15
Chronicle of Philanthropy, 7, 37, 57
The Circle of Innovation, 7
Clarke, Cheryl, 17
Coca-Cola, vi, 14
Cohn, Robin, 11
collaborating, 28-29
The Collaboration Challenge: How Nonprofits and Businesses Succeed Through Strategic Alliances, 29
Collins, James C., 7
communications audit, 4-5, 26
The Communications Network, 7
communications plan, 5, 10-11, 22-25, 62
competitive analysis, 5, 6-7, 60
Competitive Strategy, 7
Conducting a Successful Capital Campaign, 37
Conducting Successful Focus Groups, 5
congress.org, 35
Conlon, Peggy, 33
consistency, 13, 14, 15, 16, 38, 48
consultants, 5, 6, 21, 26-27, 44, 48, 49
content management system, 54
Coombs, Timothy W., 11
Coons, Patti, 45
Cops, 11
corporate spending on communications, v, vi, E
corporate sponsors, 22, 23,
Cosby, Bill, 11
cost/benefit of various vehicles, pocket
Cox, Candy, 33
Creswell, John W., 3
crisis communications, B, 61
Crisis Management, Planning for the Inevitable, 11

D

databases, 39
DDB Worldwide, 33
defining communications, v
defining media relations, 50
defining public relations, 50
Denning, Stephen, 17
Designing Brand Identity: A Complete Guide to Creating, Building, and Maintaining Strong Brands, 15
Devine, Virginia, 47
Differentiate or Die: Survival in Our Era of Killer Competition, 7
differentiation, 6-7, 12, 14
direct mail, 21, 33, 38-39, 60
Direct Marketing Association, 39
distribution plan, 10
DM News, 39
Doctors Without Borders, 14
donors
    attracting, 22, E, 28, 36, 38, 39, 40
    cultivating, 40-41
    stewarding, 22, 28, 41, 48
    timing solicitations, 39
Don't Make Me Think!: A Common Sense Approach to Web Usability, 55
Don't Mess With Texas, 16-17
Dove, Kent, 37
Dropkin, Murray, 21

E

Earle, Richard, 29
earthisland.org, 55
The Economist, v, 33
The Edna McConnell Clark Foundation, 17
Egger, Robert, 63
Eisner, Michael, 12
electronic communications, 21, 42-43
The Ellen DeGeneres Show, 11
e-mail
    building a mailing list, 43, 44, 45
    campaigns, 42-43
    challenge response system, 43
    getting your message through, 43
    listservs, 57
    pitching media, 53
    spam, 43
eModerators, 57
Emotional Branding: The New Paradigm for Connecting Brands to People, 15
e-newsletters, 42, 43
Engstrom, Ted W., 25
entertainment industry, vi, E
Entrepreneur.com, 4,
Environmental Protection Agency, 46
ePhilanthropy Foundation, 57
ephilanthropy.org, 7
event planning, 44-45, pocket
experts directory, 53
exploratorium.edu, 55

F

Fact Check, 35
Factiva, 51
The Fall of Advertising and the Rise of PR, 51
feasibility study, 36, 37
feedreader.com, 55
Fink, Steven, 11
FirstGov for Nonprofits, 7
Fitch, Brad, 51
focus groups, 2, 3, 4-5, 14, 37
Focus Groups: A Practical Guide for Applied Research, 5
Fogel, Jared, 17
Fortune 500, iv
The Foundation Center, 7
The Foundation Center's Guide to Proposal Writing, 41
foundations, 22, 23, 40, 41
Foye, Patrick, 28
Frameworks Institute, 17, 25, 35
framing, 16-17
fundraising, 22, E, 28, 36-41, 43
The Fund Raising School, 37

G

GALA: The Special Events Planner for Professionals and Volunteers, 45

Gebbie Press, 53

General Electric, vi

General Motors, vi

Getting It Printed: How to Work With Printers and Graphic Imaging Services to Assure Quality, Stay on Schedule and Control Costs, 49

Girls Inc., 29

Giving USA, 40

Gladwell, Malcolm, 43

Glander, Alison, 29

Gobe, Marc, 15

Godes, David, 47

Godin, Seth, v, 7, 43, 57

Goodheart, Ann, 49

Goodman, Andy, vii, 17, F, 45, 46

Goodwill, vi

Google, v, 3, 33, 51, 54

government agencies, 3, 28, 34, 35

government data, 3

government officials, 34-35

gracecathedral.org, 55

Graphic Designer's Digital Printing and Prepress Handbook, 49

graphic identity, *see* identity

grant writing, 36, 40, 41

Greenpeace, E

Groh, Katalina, 17

Grizzard Communications, 38

Grossman, Allen, 63

guerilla marketing, 46-47

Guerilla Marketing, 47

GuideStar, 7, 27

H

Habitat for Humanity International, 13

Handbook of Budgeting for Nonprofit Organizations, 21

Hancock, David L., 47

Hart, Ted, 57

Harvard Business Review: Crisis Management, 11

Harvard Business School Working Paper "Using Online Communication to Study Word of Mouth Communication," 47

"Hearses on the Highway," 46

"heart attack on a plate," 17

Heath, Chip, 17

Hessekiel, David, 29

High Performance Nonprofit Organizations: Managing Upstream for Greater Impact, 63

hiring communications staff, 26-27

hivstopswithme.org, 55

Home Depot, 29

Home Page Usability: 50 Homepages Deconstructed, 55

Hotmail, 43

Hot Text: Web Writing That Works, 57

Humane Methods of Slaughter Act, 47

Humane Society of America, 47

Howe, Fisher, 25

How to Measure Your Communications Program, 61

How Users Read on the Web, 57

hrc.org, 55

I

Idea Index: Graphic Effects and Typographic Treatments, 15

Idealist, 7

identity
    institutional, vi, 6
    graphic, 13, 14-15

implementation, 10

Independent Sector, 29

indybay.org, 55

Information Architecture: Blueprints for the Web, 55

Information Architecture for the World Wide Web, 55

information clutter, v

Inkindex, 7

In Search of Excellence, 7

Institute for Public Relations, 61

Internal Revenue Service, 7

International Academy of Digital Arts & Sciences, 55

An Introduction to Statistical Methods and Data Analysis, 3

investing in communications, v-vii, 20, E, 36, 37

J

JAG, 11

JAMI Charity Brands, 33

jargon, 17, 25, 41

The Jargon Files, 17

Joachimsthaler, Erich, 13

jobstar.com, 27

Judge Judy, 11

Jupiter Research, 33

K

Kenly, Eric, 49

Kerry, John, 11

keywords, 56

KFC Corporation, 46

kidshealth.org, 55

Koval, Robin, 13

Krause, Jim, 15

Krueger, Richard, 5

Krug, Steve, 55

L

Lance Armstrong Foundation, D

Lancome, 29

Late Show With David Letterman, 11

LaTouce, Bill, 21

Law and Order, 11

Lend Me Your Ears, 45

letter campaign, 35

Letts, Christine, 63

Lexis-Nexis, 51

Levinson, Jay Conrad, 47

Listening to Your Donors: The Nonprofit's Practical Guide to Designing and Conducting Surveys, 5

Lister, Gwyneth J., 39

listservs, 57

lobbying, *see* advocacy

logos, *see* identity, graphic

Lois, George, 49

Los Angeles Times, vi

Loud and Clear in an Election Year: Amplifying the Voices of Community Advocates, 35

lovemarks: The Future Beyond Brands, 15

M

Maddox, David, 21

Making and Breaking the Grid: A Graphic Design Layout Workshop, 15

Making Money While Making a Difference: How to Profit With a Nonprofit Partner, 29

Making the News: A Guide for Nonprofits and Activists, 35

marketing materials, 20, 21, 48-49, 61

marketingprofs.com, 43

market research, 3

marketresearch.com, 3

The Market Research Toolbox, 3

Mayzlin, Dina, 47

McKinsey & Co., 21

McQuarrie, Edward F., 3

measurement, 2, 10, 13, 60-61

Measuring Brand Communication ROI, 61

media
   coverage, 44, 45, 60, 61
   daybooks, 53
   deadlines, L
   distribution lists/services, 53
   "earned," 50
   ethnic, 32,
   framing news, 16-17, 34-35
   gay/lesbian, 51
   media advisories, 53
   media-friendly Web site, 53
   media relations, B, 50-53
   New California Media, 32, 51
   news releases, pocket
   pitching, 52-53
   spokespeople, B, K
   sponsorships, 29
   video news releases, 53
   week-ahead columns, 53

Media Relations Handbook for Agencies, Associations, Nonprofits and Congress, 51

message development, 16-17, 24, 36, 38, 45

Microsoft, vi

Minch, Holly, 35

Misner, Ivan R., 47

mission, 10, 11, 16, 17, 29

Morville, Peter, 55

myjewishlearning.com, 55

N

National Association of Black Journalists, 51

National Association of Hispanic Journalists, 51

National Association of Minority Media Executives, 51

The National Crime Prevention Council, D

National Gay and Lesbian Task Force, 51

National Results Council, 63

National Wildlife Federation, 29

Native American Journalists Association, 51

NCM Directory, 51

Network for Good, 7

Neumeier, Marty, 13

A New Brand World, 12

New California Media, 32, 51

newsgator.com, 55

news media, see media

News Media Yellow Book, Leadership Directories, 53

news release, see media

newstips.org, 43

The New York Times, 11, 23, 28, 32, 33, 46

Nielsen, Jakob, 55, 57

Nielsen Monitor-Plus, 11

Nielsen/Net Ratings, 55

Nike, vii, 12, 14

Nonprofit Board Answer Book, 25

The Nonprofit Handbook, 7

The Nonprofit Leadership Team, 25

The NonProfit Times, 10, 27

number of advertising messages a day, v

number of people online, 54

nyu.edu/library/resources/webwriting, 57

O

Ogilvy, David, 24

101 Ways to Boost Your Web Traffic: Internet Marketing Made Easier, 43

Ongoing Crisis Communication: Planning, Managing & Responding, 11

online advertising, see advertising

online giving, 21, 57

online-publishers.org, 43

On Philanthropy, 29, 37, 43

Oscars of the Internet, 55

Ott, R. Lyman, 3

P

partnerships, 13, 22, 23, 28-29

Paypal, 57

peer institutions, 5, 6-7, 60

People for the Ethical Treatment of Animals, 46

Peters, Tom, 6, 7

pharmaceutical industry, vi

philanthropy.com, 7, 37

Pilgrim's Pride, 46

pitching a story, see media

planned giving, 38, 39

Planned Parenthood of New England, 47

popular culture, 35, 61

Porras, Jerry I., 7

Porter, Michael, 7

PR Crisis Bible: Take Charge of the Media When All Hell Breaks Loose, 11

PR Newswire, 29

Preparing Your Capital Campaign, 37

presidential campaign, 11

Price, Jonathan and Lisa, 57

primary research, 2, 3

prnewswire.com, 53

Procter & Gamble, vi

profusion.com, 3

project brief, 20

proposal writing, 36, 40, 41

Proscio, Tony, 17

prospect research, 36, 37, 40

prsa.org, 51

Prusak, Larry, 17

prweb.com, 51

PSA Research Center at Goodwill Communications, 33

PowerPact, LLC, 29

publications, 20, 21, 48-49, 61

publicity, 50-53

public relations, 50

public-speaking.org, 45

Publishing the Nonprofit Annual Report: Tips, Traps, and Tricks of the Trade, 49

Purple Cow: Transform Your Business by Being Remarkable, v, 7

push vs. pull, 49

Q

qualitative research, *see* research

quantitative research, *see* research

questionnaires, *see* surveys

R

ranchero.com/netnewswire, 55

Red Cross, E

refining, 62-63

release forms, pocket

research
 baseline, 2, 60
 free, 3
 general, 2-8, 21
 government, 3
 primary, 2, 3, 4
 prospect research, 36, 37, 40
 qualitative, vii, viii, 3
 quantitative, vii, viii, 3, A, 6
 sample size, 3
 secondary, 2

Research Design: Qualitative, Quantitative and Mixed Methods Approaches, 3

Resource Center for Effective Corporate-Nonprofit Partnerships, 29

return on investment, v-vii, 20, 21, 24, 26

reuters.com, 53

Ries, Al and Laura Ries, 13, 51

Rivkin, Steve, 7

Roberts, Kevin, 15

Rosenfeld, Louis, 55

Ross, Bernard, 63

Rusch, Robin, 13

Rutenberg, Jim, 11

Ryan, William P., 63

S

Safire, William, 45

salaries, 27

salary.com, 27

salarysource.com, 27

Salzman, Jason, 35

Samara, Timothy, 15

Schmittlein, David, 43

Schultz, Don E., 61

The Secrets of Master Marketing: Discover How to Produce an Endless Stream of New, Repeat and Referral Business by Using These Powerful Marketing and Customer Service Secrets, 47

search engine optimization, 54, 56-57

searchenginestrategies.biz/index.htm, 57

searchenginewatch.com, 57

Segal, Clare, 63

Selling the Invisible: A Field Guide to Modern Marketing, 5

SEMPO, 57

Shim, Jae K., 21

Sidles, Constance, 49

Simon, Judith Sharken, 5

Sinickas, Angela, 61

slogans, 14, D

The Society of Publication Designers 39th Publication Design Annual, 49

Solomon, Jeff, 57

spam, 43, 56

Special Events: Proven Strategies for Nonprofit Fundraising, 45

speechwriting, 45

Spider-Man, E

SPIN Works, 51

spinproject.org, 51

spokespeople, B, K

Springboard: How Storytelling Ignites Action in Knowledge-Era Organizations, 17

Stanford Social Innovation Review, 17

Starbucks, 12, 29

statistical accuracy, vii, 3

Steckel, Richard, 29

Stein, Ben, 10

Sturtevant, William, 41

stewardship, *see* donors

storytelling, 17

Storytelling as Best Practice, 17

Storytelling for Grantseekers: Telling Your Organization's Story, 17

Storytelling in Organizations: How Narrative and Storytelling Are Transforming 21st Century Management, 17

style guide, 15, pocket

Subway, 17

surveys
 accuracy, vii, 3
 e-mail, 3, 4
 general, 3, 4, 6, 26, 60, 61
 in person, 3, 4
 low-cost, 3
 mail, 3, 4
 process, 3, 4
 questions, 5
 sample, pocket
 telephone, 3, 4, 6
 Web, 3, 4

SWOT analysis, pocket

T

Tahir, Marie, 55

targeting your audience, *see* audience

Taylor, Caroline, 49

Techsoup, 7

testing
 awareness testing, 24
 before-and-after testing, 60
 campaign goal, 36, 37
 identity, 4-5, 14
 materials, 4-5, 14, 38, 60
 messages, 4-5, 14, 16, 38, 60
 Web sites, 55

Thaler, Linda Kaplan, 13

thank yous, 41, 45

ThinkLogic LLC, 57

tolerance.org, 55

Tom's of Maine, 6
tracking
   media coverage, 51, 60, 61
   Web usage, 61
Transforming Qualitative Data: Description, Analysis and Interpretation, 3
Trout, Jack, 7
TheTruth.com, 17
The 22 Immutable Laws of Branding, 13

U

United Negro College Fund, D
The United States Fund for Unicef, 23
United States Postal Service, 39
United Way of Long Island, 28
university libraries, 2, 3
University of Pennsylvania, 35
Unleashing the Idea Virus, 43
usability testing, 55, 56
useit.com, 57
U.S. Census Bureau, 51
U.S. Congress, 35
U.S. News and World Report, 50, 60

V

Van Auken, Brad, 13
viral marketing, I
volunteers, 22, 23, 52

W

The Wall Street Journal, 21
Walters, Jeffrey S., 61
Wanamaker, John, 32
Webby Awards, 55
webclipping.com, 51
Web Marketing Today, I
Web sites
   as strategic tool, 10
   blogs, 55
   content management system, 54
   general, 54-57
   search engine optimization, 54, 56-57
   usability testing, 55, 56
Wendroff, Alan L., 45

The West Wing, 52
Wharton School of Business, 43
whatworks.org, 7
Wheele, Alina, 15
Why Bad Ads Happen to Good Causes, F
wilder.org, 5
Winfrey, Oprah, 48
Winning Grants Step-by-Step: The Complete Workbook for Planning, Developing and Writing Successful Proposals, 41
Wisconsin Advertising Project, 11
Wodtke, Christina, 55
Wolcott, Harry F., 3
Wong, Thomas, 43
word of mouth advertising, 46, 47, 62
The World's Best Known Marketing Secret: Building Your Business With Word-Of-Mouth Marketing, 47
Writing for a Good Cause: The Complete Guide to Crafting Proposals and Other Persuasive Pieces for Nonprofits, 41

Y

Yale School of Management, 47
Yahoo!, 33
Yum Brands, 46

COST-AND-BENEFIT CHART OF SELECT MEDIA

Matching the right tools to the right job takes some planning. The following cost/benefit analysis chart will give you some ideas about the cost, reach and best use of various media. It's all about finding the most effective ways of reaching your target audiences with the appropriate media for your message and within your budget.

Some organizations will be heavy on high-end fundraising communications, especially if they're launching a major capital campaign. Others will emphasize mass media, including advertising and/or publicity. If you're going to make the kind of significant investment an advertising campaign entails, you've got to be sure you have enough money in your budget to support the kind of repetition and longevity necessary to be effective.

For more details about individual communications tools, please refer to Chapter Four.

VEHICLE	REACH	COST	BEST USE
Annual report	targeted	high	stewarding and attracting donors, foundations, partners, etc.
Donor or membership newsletter	targeted	low to mid	stewarding and attracting donors/constituents
Magazine	targeted	mid to high	building awareness/stewarding and attracting partners, etc.
Event/major (black-tie fundraiser, major conference)	targeted	high	stewarding and attracting donors, partners, media
Event/minor (open house, lecture, etc.)	targeted/ general population	low	attract new constituents, donors
Case for support	targeted	high	attract donors and prospects
Direct-mail appeal	targeted	low to high	attract donors
Web site	general population	low to high	promotional/informational
E-newsletter	targeted	low	reach constituents, donors
Viral marketing	general population	low	reach new supporters and constituents
National media distribution	media/general population	low to mid	building awareness/reaching new audiences
Video news release	general population	mid	building awareness/best for small to mid-sized markets
Public opinion poll	general population	mid to high	benchmarking/testing
Advertising/print	general population (unless specialty publication)	mid to high	building awareness/reaching new audiences
Advertising/TV	general population	high	building awareness/reaching new audiences
Advertising/cable	more targeted than broadcast	mid to high	building awareness/reaching new audiences
Advertising/radio	general population	mid	building awareness/reaching new audiences
Window displays, bumper stickers, etc.	general population	low	reaching new supporters and constituents

COMMUNICATIONS TOOLKIT *A guide to navigating communications for the nonprofit world*   causecommunications.org

CREATIVE BRIEF

Client Name

Name

Project Name

Project 123

Purpose/Marketing Objective

Objective (what we want the communications piece to do):
    To build awareness, to increase donations by X%, reach new donors (what's your goal?)
Example:
    This ad should introduce the reader to key ABC Nonprofit services, history of success

Targets

Primary Audience: Age, Gender, Income
Secondary Audience: Age, Gender, Income

Call to Action

What do you want the target audience to do (donate, call congressperson, etc.)?

Key Benefits

What are the key benefits to be included in the piece? What copy facts would you like to include?

Tone/Look and Feel

Input on what you'd like the creative team to be mindful of as it develops a look and feel.

Mandatories

What elements must be included in every ad – logo, 800 number and graphic standards that must be observed at all times?

Additional Research/Background

Other information about your organization that would help the creative team more fully understand the challenges.

Formats Required

For example, if the project is an ad, note the number of formats this ad will need to be adapted to – full page, half page, etc. Also note if you'd need to have this in e-format, etc.

Deadlines

Significant deadlines – these range from internal presentations to material deadlines for publications.

EVENT-PLANNING CHECKLIST

Use the following as a starting point to develop a checklist that is appropriate for the type and scale of event you are hosting:

- ❏ Fundraising goal
- ❏ Budget
- ❏ Audience (invitation-only, general public, etc.)
- ❏ Venue
- ❏ Number of attendees
- ❏ Type of invitation (elegant, simple, flyer, ad)
- ❏ Admission (ticket, free)
- ❏ Sponsorships
- ❏ Photographer/videographer
- ❏ Save-the-date card
- ❏ Printed program
- ❏ Publicity
- ❏ Staffing
- ❏ Schedule of activities
- ❏ Seating plans/table schematics
- ❏ Rentals (tables, chairs, linens, stage, equipment, umbrellas, generator, tents)
- ❏ AV and other technical equipment (lighting, sound, two-way radios, webcast)
- ❏ Stage/podium
- ❏ Parking/valet
- ❏ Security/fire marshal
- ❏ Limos for VIP guests/speakers
- ❏ Signs/banners
- ❏ Décor
- ❏ Florist
- ❏ Caterer/bar
- ❏ Check-in tables/coat check
- ❏ Handouts/gifts
- ❏ Cleanup crew

NEWS RELEASE GUIDELINES

Your release should look like a news release, with a bold headline, proper formatting, complete information, no grammatical or spelling errors and, most importantly, newsworthy content. Most news media use the *Associated Press Stylebook*; your release will be viewed more favorably if you follow its copy-editing rules. You also may want to release your news in more than one language, depending on your audience.

Keep in mind the following guidelines:

FORMATTING

- Use 8-1/2x11-inch paper with at least one-inch margins.
- Use only one side of each sheet of paper.
- Start the page with FOR IMMEDIATE RELEASE and the date.
- If you are releasing news in advance of the official announcement, indicate that the release is "embargoed" until a certain date and time.
- Include complete contact information.
- List the city, state and date at the beginning of the first line, followed by two dashes.
- Include all critical information, especially "who, what, when, where, why and how."
- Don't break a paragraph at the end of a page.
- Center the word "more" surrounded by two dashes at the bottom of the page to indicate the release continues.
- At the top of the next page, include a shortened version of the headline and the page number.
- At the end of the release, include a short paragraph about the organization (or specific program) and its history.
- Indicate the end of the release by centering either -- # # # -- or -- 30 -- at the bottom of the last page.

CONTENT

A release should be written like a news story, following an inverted pyramid structure, with the most important information at the top. Most editors scan the headline and lead paragraph; if the release doesn't grab them, they toss it. Some publications and Web sites may run your release verbatim but may have to shorten it to fit the available space. They usually cut from the bottom.

PHOTO/VIDEO RELEASE FORM

I, _____, consent to the unrestricted use, by ABC Nonprofit Organization (and those acting with its permission and authority), of any and all photographs taken, in whole or in part, unlimited use, for all purposes in any form or medium, including, without limitation, its use through or on any electronic media, including the Internet.

I waive any right to inspect or approve the finished product or products or the advertising copy or printed matter that may be used with the finished photograph(s).

Further, I relinquish all rights, titles and interests I may have in the finished photograph(s), negative(s) and reproduction to any responsible business firm or publication. It is understood that ABC Nonprofit Organization retains copyright of images at all times under the express understanding and agreement that ABC Nonprofit Organization shall have exclusive reproduction rights to the images.

I hereby release ABC Nonprofit Organization from any and all claims in connection with the photograph(s), including any and all claims of libel.

_____ I am over the age of 18. I have read the above and fully understand its contents.

_____ I am the parent or guardian of a minor. I have read the above and fully understand its contents. I hereby grant permission for my child's/ward's photograph(s) to be used in the manner specified above.

Name (please print) _____ Age _____

Minor's Name(s) if applicable _____

Address/City/State/Zip _____

_____

Telephone _____ E-mail _____

Signature _____ Date _____

Relation to subject (if subject is a minor) _____

COMMUNICATIONS TOOLKIT *A guide to navigating communications for the nonprofit world*   causecommunications.org

1234 Any Street | Any Town, USA 98765 | **T** 310.458.2823 | **F** 310.656.0613 | **www.abcnonprofit.org**

SAMPLE CAMPAIGN STYLE GUIDE

This example of a style guide shows how you can create a unified communications campaign using various marketing tools.

Print Ads

Direct Mail

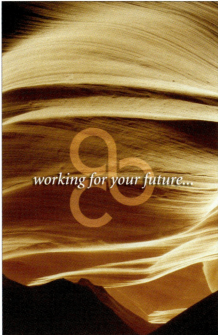

Posters

COMMUNICATIONS TOOLKIT *A guide to navigating communications for the nonprofit world*

causecommunications.org

1234 Any Street | Any Town, USA 98765 | T 310.458.2823 | F 310.656.0613 | www.abcnonprofit.org

SAMPLE COMMUNICATIONS SURVEY

1. How often do you hear information/news about ABC? Circle one:

   1/week   2/month   1/quarter   1/year   Other   Never

2. How often do you want to hear news/information about ABC? Circle one:

   1/week   2/month   1/quarter   1/year   Other   Never

3. Are you satisfied with the way ABC communicates with you about work in progress, activities and achievements? Circle one:

   Yes   No

4. What are your main sources of news about ABC? (rated on a sliding scale of 1 = Infrequent and 5 = Frequent)

Advertising						
Radio	5	4	3	2	1	N/A
Print	5	4	3	2	1	N/A
Direct Mail	5	4	3	2	1	N/A
Media Stories	5	4	3	2	1	N/A
Newsletters	5	4	3	2	1	N/A
Annual Report	5	4	3	2	1	N/A
Website	5	4	3	2	1	N/A
E-Communications	5	4	3	2	1	N/A
Sponsorships	5	4	3	2	1	N/A

5. What was the most memorable/most effective communications effort that ABC has undertaken? Circle one:

   Radio Advertising   **Annual Report**
   Print Advertising   **Web site**
   Direct Mail   **E-Communications**
   Media Stories   **Sponsorships/Events**
   Newsletters   **N/A**

6. How does news about ABC reach you? Circle one:

   Radio Advertising   **Annual Report**
   Print Advertising   **Web site**
   Direct Mail   **E-Communications**
   Media Stories   **Sponsorships/Events**
   Newsletters   **N/A**

7. What is your preferred way of learning about ABC events and news? Circle one:

   Radio Advertising   **Annual Report**
   Print Advertising   **Web site**
   Direct Mail   **E-Communications**
   Media Stories   **Sponsorships/Events**
   Newsletters   **N/A**

8. What communications tools does ABC use that could be more effective? Circle one:

   Radio Advertising   **Annual Report**
   Print Advertising   **Web site**
   Direct Mail   **E-Communications**
   Media Stories   **Sponsorships/Events**
   Newsletters   **N/A**

9. What other nonprofits do you feel communicate well about their activities and achievements?

   _____
   _____
   _____
   _____

10. What do you expect from ABC's communications efforts?

    _____
    _____
    _____
    _____

11. What is ABC not doing (from a communications standpoint) that you would like to see it do?

    _____
    _____
    _____
    _____

COMMUNICATIONS TOOLKIT *A guide to navigating communications for the nonprofit world*

causecommunications.org

SAMPLE IDENTITY GUIDELINES

The ABC logo/logotype is a key element of our organizational identity. The symbol signifies the importance of a collaborative effort in our organization. As such, the ABC logo is designed to clearly identify ABC. The logo is an important aspect of how ABC is perceived. Consistent use of the logo will ensure its strength and long-term recognition. If we work together to control use of our identity, we will begin to be perceived as one entity. These guidelines are intended to introduce the new logo/logotype and to suggest guidelines for its proper use.

2-COLOR LOGO
The preferred usage of the logo is with our two corporate colors. The logomark appears in Teal PMS 3282. The logotype appears in black. The ABC logo consists of the logomark and logotype. These elements must never be separated.

1-COLOR LOGO
The logomark and logotype should be Teal PMS 3282 with the logomark screened at 60 percent and the logotype at 100 percent OR the logomark and logotype should be black with the logomark screened at 60 percent and the logotype at 100 percent.

LOGO SIZE
Please limit use of the ABC logo to these three sizes: 3/4", 1", 1-3/8".

CLEAR SPACE
The logo must always be clear of any competing visuals. There must be at least half the height (1/2 y) of an entire logo (y) as clear space around the logo. This gives the logo room to be set apart, enhancing readability.

REVERSING OUR LOGO
Simply reverse to solid white out of solid color backgrounds only. Do not screen or alter in any way.

OUR COLORS
Color is also a vital component of the ABC identity program. When consistently applied, it will serve to strengthen the communicative impact. Only these colors are approved for use on the logo. The CMYK breakdown shown below should only be used when printing process color.

UNACCEPTABLE LOGO USAGE
Never break apart the logomark from the logotype, unless using the mark as a design element screened in the background.

Never break the components of the logomark away from each other or the logotype.

Never change the position of the logomark and logotype.

Never change the typeface or type size used in the logotype.

Never change the size of the logomark or logotype.

SWOT ANALYSIS FORM

Photocopy several copies of this SWOT, strengths, weaknesses, opportunities and threats, chart and fill in the blanks for your organization and your peer institutions. Be candid in your assessment and periodically re-evaluate your standing, especially when your nonprofit has gone through a major organizational change.

	YOU	COMPETITOR
STRENGTHS		
WEAKNESSES		
OPPORTUNITIES		
THREATS (AKA CHALLENGES)		

COMMUNICATIONS TOOLKIT *A guide to navigating communications for the nonprofit world*   causecommunications.org

Cause Communications
1336 Fifth Street
Santa Monica, CA 90401-1415
www.causecommunications.org

Dear Reader,

We are pleased to send you a copy of "Communications Toolkit – A guide to navigating communications for the nonprofit world." We are hopeful this book will help your organization increase awareness and funds by developing well-crafted communications.

It is our sincere hope that this toolkit will serve as a helpful resource in your quest for communication perfection, and that you will refer to it often.

And please let us know your thoughts. We plan to update the content of this toolkit on a regular basis. Your feedback will ensure future editions reflect the most current communications needs of the nonprofit sector. Please forward your comments to toolkit@causecommunications.org.

Sincerely,

Andrew Posey
Vice President